FORECASTING PROFITS
USING PRICE & TIME

Wiley Trader's Exchange Series

William Blau, *Momentum, Direction, and Divergence*

John F. Ehlers, *MESA and Trading Market Cycles*

Mark Etzkorn, *Trading with Oscillators*

Robert Fischer, *Fibonacci Applications and Strategies for Traders*

Ed Gately, *Neural Networks for Financing Forecasting*

Ed Gately, *Forecasting Profits Using Price & Time*

Gary Klopfenstein and Jon Stein, *Trading Currency Cross Rates*

Robert Pardo, *Design, Testing, and Optimization of Trading Systems*

John Sweeney, *Maximum Adverse Excursion*

FORECASTING PROFITS USING PRICE & TIME

ED GATELY

JOHN WILEY & SONS, INC.

New York • Chichester • Weinheim • Brisbane • Singapore • Toronto

Copyright © 1998 by Ed Gately.
Published by John Wiley & Sons, Inc.

Library of Congress Cataloging in Publication Data:

ISBN 0-471-15539-X

Printed in the United States of America
10   9   8   7   6   5   4   3   2   1

To
Ted Gately and Joe Norris
who have always been there when I needed them—thank you both.

PREFACE

———

Trading securities, futures contracts, indexes, currencies, and agricultural products is a risky business at best. The ability to set goals or targets that might be reached in the future helps to take some of the risk out of the transaction, because if the price moves away from the target we are able to take corrective action. Risk can be further reduced by not only setting targets, but by confirming the proposed price movement by establishing the probable movement using technical analysis.

Although this text does cover a number of technical analysis tools, it is not intended to replace the excellent texts by John Murphy, Martin Pring, and many others. The chapters on technical analysis are intended to acquaint newcomers to the basics of technical analysis and to show how oscillators and moving averages can be combined with various channels to gain a workable, relatively risk-free technique.

ED GATELY

Mahwah, New Jersey
December 1997

ACKNOWLEDGMENTS

———

I thank the following people who have contributed directly and indirectly to the writing of this book:

My wife, Susan, who did the first editing of the completed copy.

Eddie Kwong of Kasanjian Research wrote the manual on which Chapter 8 is based. He also reviewed Chapter 6 and made many excellent suggestions on how it could be improved.

My step-daughter, Anita Greiter, who compiled the bibliography; a major undertaking, I might add.

Pamela van Giessen, my editor at John Wiley & Sons, who has been very helpful in a variety of ways.

E. G.

CONTENTS

CHAPTER 1

The Importance of Targets   1

CHAPTER 2

Fundamental Methods   7

CHAPTER 3

Technical Methods for Setting Time and
Price Targets   33

CHAPTER 4

Oscillators   63

CHAPTER 5

Other Patterns and Events   77

CHAPTER 6

Using Fibonacci and Other Number Series to Establish
Price and Time Targets   89

CHAPTER 7

Positioning a Stop-Loss and Profit Objective   107

CHAPTER 8

The Bradley Model: Guidance from the Stars?   119

CHAPTER 9

Using Neural Networks and Genetic Algorithms to Establish
Time and Price Targets   127

CHAPTER 10

Putting It Together: Utilizing a Variety
of Techniques   133

APPENDIX

Software Used in Writing This Book   141

BIBLIOGRAPHY
143

INDEX
161

1

THE IMPORTANCE OF TARGETS

TULIPOMANIA OR THE MADNESS OF CROWDS

In 1841 Charles Mackay published his book *Extraordinary Popular Delusions and the Madness of Crowds,* in which he explores a number of financial disasters created by the actions of crowds of people. Probably the most famous of these disasters was *Tulipomania*, where people in Holland bid the price of tulip bulbs to astronomical prices, only to have the price plummet back to a rational level. Crowd psychology also produced the stock market crash of 1929, where stock prices were bid to extremes, only to have them all come tumbling down. History shows that these situations are not unique, and, Mackay in his book covers "The Mississippi Scheme," "The South Sea Bubble," and "The Crusades." One thing is certain, the speculative bubble *always* bursts, leaving many "investors" (read "speculators") penniless.

The actions of crowds have been described as the *Greater Fool Theory,* which goes as follows: If I buy something at an inflated price, then I am a fool, but will be okay when I want to sell it as long as I can find a greater fool who will pay me more for the item than I paid. When no more greater fools can be found, the price stops rising, and everyone

---

Author's Note: *Extraordinary Popular Delusions and the Madness of Crowds* has been in print since 1841, ranking it among the oldest continuously available books.

tries to cash in their profits. Since no one wants to buy, the price comes crashing down.

Bernard Baruch wrote, in the foreword to the 1932 edition of *Extraordinary Popular Delusions and the Madness of Crowds,* "All economic movements, by their very nature, are motivated by crowd psychology . . . . Anyone taken as an individual is tolerably sensible and reasonable—as a member of a crowd, he at once becomes a blockhead."

Prices on the stock and commodity markets are in constant motion and apparently chaotic; they can run up very quickly, and back down even faster. It is a rare event when a trading day is so quiet that the daily open, high, low, and close prices are all the same. It is much more likely to see an unaccountable price jump, or an apparently irrational gain following a poor press release. All this seemingly random motion does, as we will see, have a sense to it. It is due to the crowd effect.

CROWDS AND THE MARKET

A business needs money, so it sells stock. A retiring couple sell their bigger-than-necessary house and move to an apartment, leaving a large amount of money to be invested, so they buy some stock. A widow gets an insurance check and uses it to buy more shares in a mutual fund. A middle-aged man decides to open a business, so he liquidates some of his stock to have available cash. It is these types of transactions, multiplied by millions of events, that cause the bulk of price changes in the markets. This group of people, each one acting for personal reasons, constitutes a crowd.

Bad news causes a rush to sell, and the price goes down. If the news is bad enough, the price "gaps" down. A downward gap on the chart occurs when the next price is below the previous low, as in Figure 1-1. Gaps usually occur on openings. An upward gap is an open above the previous day's high. Usually, bad news causes selling to overshoot, buy orders come in, and the price rises some and stabilizes at some new price. That is, equilibrium is established. In the case of good news, buy orders flood the market resulting in a price rise. If the rise is sufficient, then profit taking occurs, and the price falls slightly as a new equilibrium is established.

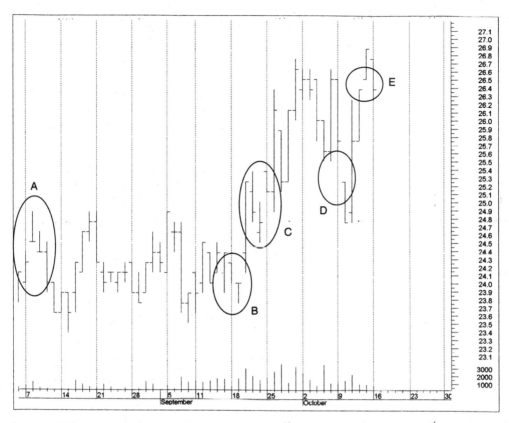

Figure 1-1 Daily plot of A. G. Edwards stock. During this 2½ month period there were five gaps. Four of the gaps were up (Points A, B, C, and E) and one was down (Point D).

Figure 1-1 shows four upward gaps (A, B, C, E) and one downward gap at D. Gaps rarely occur on charts longer than daily. They usually occur on the open, and on a weekly chart the probable day for a gap to occur would be on Monday's open. Figure 1-2 is a weekly chart of the same stock covering approximately 2 years. Here there are only two gaps. Notice that there were five gaps in a 2½-month period using daily plots and only two gaps in a span of nearly 2 years using a weekly plot.

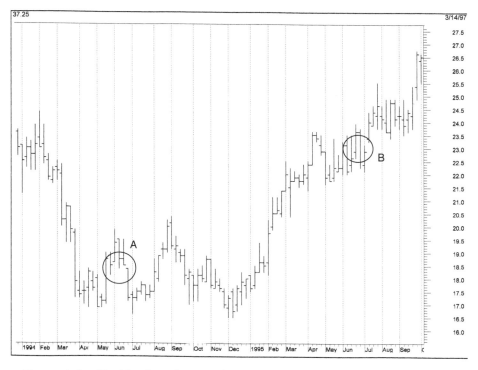

Figure 1-2   Weekly plot of A. G. Edwards stock—compare to daily plot shown in Figure 1-1. During the nearly 2-year period covered there are only two gaps (Points A and B). This occurred because the price gapped up on a Monday. Gaps on the rest of the days of the week do not show on a weekly plot.

SETTING PRICE AND TIME TARGETS

It is by setting price targets and time targets that we can anticipate how big the move may be and when it might take place. If we do not set targets, then we are merely *followers*. For example, if we target that the stock price can rise from $10.00 to $12.00, at which point there will be some profit taking, then we can anticipate this event and be among the profit takers by putting in a sell stop at $12.00.

Most forms of chart analysis and technical analysis are attempts to measure the demand for a stock or commodity; that is, to predict whether the price will go up or down and, by using certain indicators, how far the price will move. We call this the *magnitude* of the move.

Other technical analysis, for example, cycle and Fibonacci analysis, is used to establish the time at which a change in trend will occur. We refer to this as the *duration* of the move.

At this time we must stress the importance of establishing not only the probable direction the price of a security will move, but also the probable price and time targets on a continual basis. Because the targets are based on the initial conditions, and these conditions continually change, it is essential that the targets be reevaluated on a regular or periodic basis.

It is possible to invest in the markets without setting price and time targets, as is the case with popular trend-following methods. However, the risk of large equity fluctuations is greater when targets are not used. For example, even a plan with a target that falls short of its goal may produce better performance on a risk basis than a program without targets. Option traders know that it is almost impossible to make money buying or selling options without having very carefully defined price and time targets,

Targets improve performance by getting you out of the market before a turn. Although you fall short of maximizing return, you can greatly reduce the equity swings. Also, targets imply being out of the market more, not panicking at the time of exit, not fighting the crowds.

It is not unusual to have more than one target for a given security. One target may be a short term, intended to be reached during the next month, while a second target may not be achievable until next year.

In the following chapters we discuss a variety of methods to set both price and time targets.

2

FUNDAMENTAL METHODS

Future price movements can be forecast using fundamental analysis or technical analysis. Fundamental analysis incorporates events that impact the market and can be used to estimate future price movement. Technical analysis uses past prices to foretell future prices. This chapter shows ways of using fundamental analysis to forecast future price movements of securities and for establishing when the move will occur.

LINKAGES

Many economic events are linked; that is, what happens to one part of the economy, market, or security affects some other elements in the economy. By studying these relationships, we can target when, by how much, and in what direction a security's price may move.

It is accepted that interest rate yields and the stock market are linked, and that the bond market leads the stock market. Thus, if it is widely believed that the Federal Reserve will lower interest rates, then bond prices will rise in anticipation of a rate cut. Most often, the purpose of lowering rates is to stimulate the economy; therefore, a rise in the stock market will also follow. If we can estimate how much interest rates will fall, and compare what happened in the past under similar circumstances, we can then approximate how much the stock market might rise. Considering that the Federal Reserve (Fed) meets during the third week of the month, we can expect the markets will begin to move in the first two weeks of the month in anticipation of a decision to lower interest rates. Depending on the size of the anticipated move, the market may or may not make an additional move after the announcement. Thus, we are able to determine a time window in which the market should move. The study of how the bond and stock markets reacted to other rate cuts allows us to estimate how far the markets might move if the interest rates are cut. In other words, we are able to *target* the new price.

It is important to keep a certain perspective. If the corrective action of the Fed is to lower interest rates following six previous interest rate rises, the market reaction will be much greater than if it comes after six other rate cuts. The first rate cut, after a series of increases, is recognized by the market as a change in policy and often causes much more of a reaction than if it is just a continuation of the existing trend.

Precious metal prices are also considered as "linked"; for example, the prices of gold, platinum, and silver tend to move together. A 10-percent change in the price of gold usually causes a 5- to 15-percent change in the price of platinum and silver. Similarly, if platinum moves 10 percent, it usually causes gold and silver to move 5 to 15 percent. A 10-percent move in silver has less effect on the price of gold and platinum.

The price of soybeans is linked to the prices of corn and wheat, because each may be used as feed for livestock, based on their protein content (and other factors). In turn, the prices of cattle and hogs are linked to the prices of soybeans, corn, and wheat. Thus the threat of a drought might drive up the price of soybeans and corn, which in turn will drive up the price of wheat, which in turn will drive up the price of livestock.

These feedgrain linkages are illustrated in Figures 2-1 to 2-6, charts covering soybeans, soybean meal, soybean oil, cattle, corn, and wheat. Notice how much these charts look alike. Note that wheat is harvested in May, yet its price rises are entirely driven by corn and beans. Figure 2-4 shows a rise in cattle prices based on the cost of feed. Although the new crop will not be used to feed cattle for December delivery, anticipated higher prices effect a rise in currently stored grain.

The economy has thousands of market linkages. For example, if the price of steel goes up, the cost of automobile manufacturing increases.

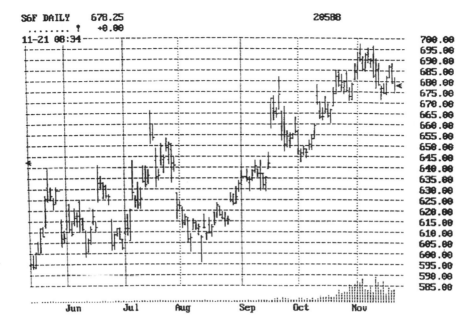

Figure 2-1 Soybean futures.

Figure 2-2 Soybean meal futures.

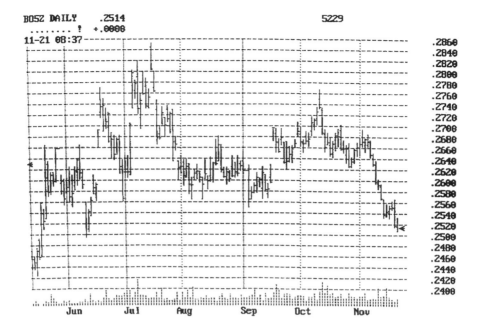

Figure 2-3 Soybean oil futures.

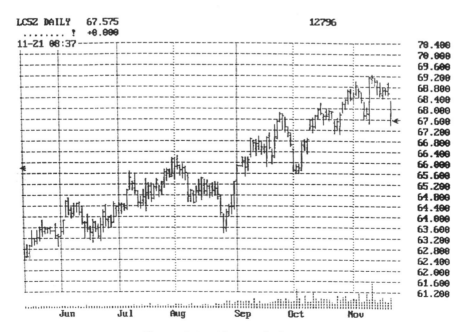

Figure 2-4 Live cattle futures.

Figure 2-5   Corn futures.

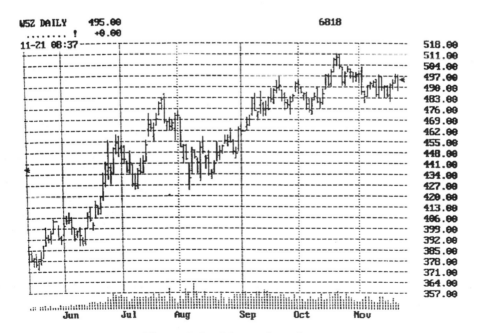

Figure 2-6   Winter wheat futures.

11

Assuming that the car companies cannot pass on part or all of the cost increase to consumers, or that a price increase meets resistant buyers, automobile companies make less money and the stock goes down.

There is a relationship among most major currencies. Some of these links are loose, such as the dollar/deutsche mark (DM) and dollar/yen link. When the news is dollar-related, both the yen and mark may have similar reactions, but when the significant change is reflected in the Japanese economy, the $/DM relationship may behave very differently. The way the U.S. economy is affected by Japanese policy may be quite different from its effect on Germany. This is particularly true when the policy involves U.S. trade quotas.

A tight relationship exists among the continental European currencies. The Danish and Swedish kroner track the deutsche mark as though they were all the same currency, because their economies are interdependent in many ways and they share a common heritage. The French franc tracks the mark more loosely than the kroner, because these economies are only slightly linked and their cultures and heritage are very different. These relationships allow us to forecast to a lesser or greater degree, and with a varying amount of confidence, what will happen. If the deutsche mark goes up, we can expect that the Danish and Swedish kroner will follow closely behind, but not necessarily the French franc.

EARNINGS, NEW PRODUCT, MERGERS, AND OTHER ANNOUNCEMENTS

A number of expected and unexpected events can affect the price of a stock, such as anticipated earnings, new products, possible mergers, and other news. While the entire stock market tends to move with the economy, individual stock prices are closely tied to earnings. The ratio of the stock price to its earnings is a measure of the rate at which the company and its earnings are expected to grow. High-technology companies that are growing rapidly, such as Intel and Microsoft, carry high price-to-earnings ratios. Companies with limited growth prospects possess small ratios; those in contracting industries have even smaller ratios.

Zacks and Standard & Poor's estimate the quarterly earnings of all major companies. A company that does not meet the "Street's" estimate will find its stock down sharply on the announcement of its true earnings. A company that exceeds its earning's forecast will find its stock up sharply. Knowledge of the true and estimated earnings of a company therefore can lead to large trading profits. Fortunately, all people who would know the exact figures are corporate insiders who are barred from trading ahead of this information.

The announcements about new products can also move stock prices. Most announcements are intended to push the stock price upwards. If the new product represents a breakthrough in technology, then the upward move can be quite dramatic. An announcement about a merger, purchase of a business, sale of a division, or other asset sale can all affect the stock price. The direction of the movement will depend on the effect of the announcement on future earnings.

Other events can affect a stock's price. For example, the government ban on DDT led to the manufacturers taking a one-time charge for the discontinued business.

REGRESSION ANALYSIS

Studying how far a price is from some normal value often gives clues to when to expect changes in trend. Regression analysis, sometimes called least-squares analysis, can be thought of as a way of determining the best straight line through a series of data points. This technique minimizes the distances between the prices and the resulting trendline. Figure 2-7 shows a historical plot of a stock price with a regression line plotted through the data. Prices are evenly distributed on both sides of the regression line.

Notice that during this trending period, prices fluctuated a similar amount above and below the regression line. In this case, once the price moved approximately 1½ points above or below the regression line, it reversed direction. In essence, we could say that the prices oscillated about the regression line.

Figure 2-8 is a weekly plot of Boatmans Bank stock over a 4½-year span. Here two regression lines have been drawn: one from April

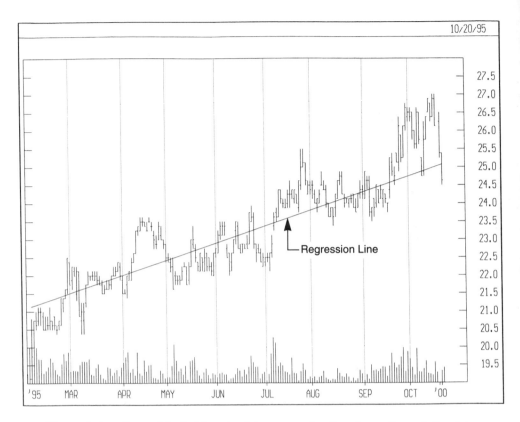

Figure 2-7   Chart of A. G. Edwards with a regression line drawn through the data.

1992 to September 1994, a period of $2\frac{1}{2}$ years; the second from November 1994 to January 1996, a period of $1\frac{1}{4}$ years. This chart shows that regression analysis is applicable to weekly as well as daily charts.

Figure 2-9 is similar to Figure 2-8, but with a shorter-term view of the regression analysis, having six regression lines rather than the two shown in Figure 2-8.

The fact that the data stay within a given distance from the regression line means that we can use these amounts as targets for buying and selling. That is, buy when the price is at the distance below the regression line; sell when the price is at the distance above the regression line.

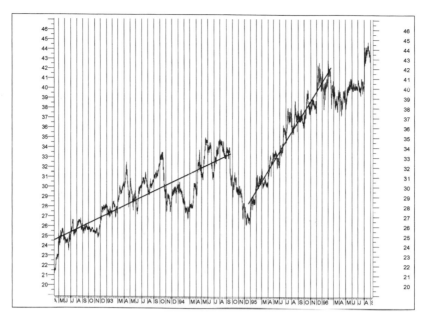

Figure 2-8 Chart of Boatmans Bank with regression lines drawn through two different time periods.

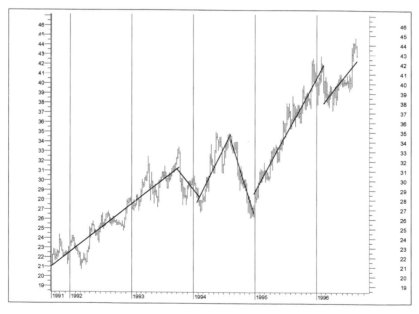

Figure 2-9 Chart of Boatmans Bank with regression lines drawn through six different time periods.

SEASONALITY

We can take advantage of natural phenomena and fundamentals to help identify targets. Seasonality can be used to identify potential changes in trend. Usually the price of grains drops at harvest time, and the price of fuel oil rises as winter approaches. Therefore, the harvest signals that hedged accounts in crops should exit shorts, while late summer requires a shift to the long side of fuel oil.

Figure 2-10 is a weekly chart of winter wheat from mid-1990 through most of 1995. Note that the points marked A on the chart are the yearly lows, and that they occur in the middle of the year when the harvest is nearly complete and good assessment of yield can be made. The points marked B are the high points for the year. Notice that these occur around the first of the year when it is impossible to estimate the coming harvest, and existing inventory is being drawn down rapidly.

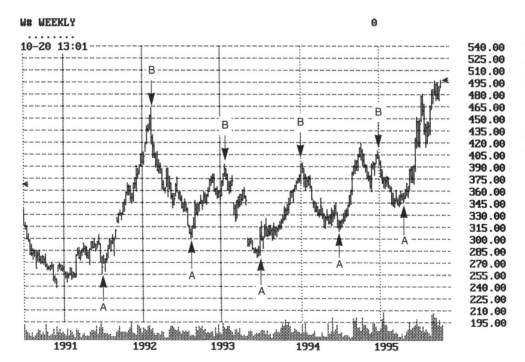

Figure 2-10   Chart of wheat with the highs and lows marked.

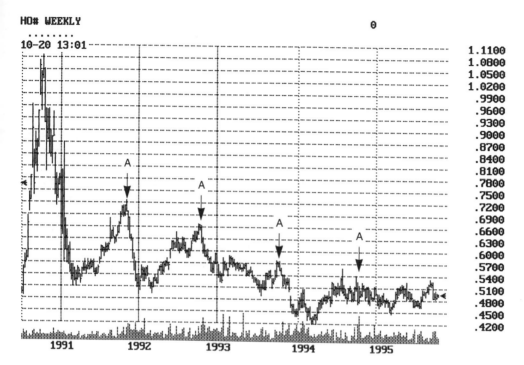

Figure 2-11   Chart of heating oil with the highs and lows marked.

The harvest of winter wheat in the southern states is probably the catalyst that starts the market down again.

The price of heating oil is shown in Figure 2-11. The points marked A represent yearly highs. Observe that these peaks occur in the fall when concern of the severity of the coming winter is at its highest, yet there is little information.

CONVENTIONAL CYCLES

Cycles are another intrinsic component of price movement and can be very helpful in determining when a change in trend might take place. Cycles allow us to accurately predict events in nature: bird migrations, the tides, and planetary movements. Cycle analysis can be used to predict changes in the financial markets, although not normally with the accuracy found in nature. As expected, most commodity price cycles are tied to seasonality, which is clearly a subset of cycles. Some stock prices are linked to the seasonal cycles. This is most common for companies whose primary products are agricultural or whose services are themselves seasonal. Other stock prices are linked to the cycles of new product introductions.

One simple way of finding cycles is to use the popular *Metastock*™ software program, which has a subprogram to locate possible cycles. After the program has been given the number of days (week, months) to use, it draws the lines on the chart and the mouse can be used to move the lines to see various fits. By trying different periods and moving the lines around, a best fit can be achieved. Figure 2-12 shows a

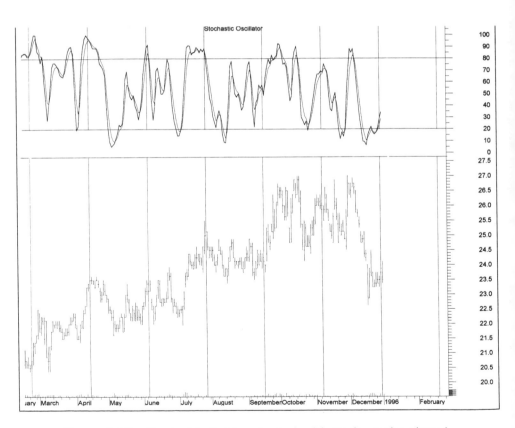

Figure 2-12   Chart of A. G. Edwards stock with 36-day cycles plotted.

chart of A. G. Edwards with 36-day cycle lines fitted to the chart. The *stochastic oscillator* is an oscillator that shows when a security is oversold or overbought. When the oscillator is a low value, the security is oversold, and when it has a high value, the security is overbought. Notice that the cycle lines are located where the stochastic oscillator is making major changes. When a cycle has been found, the *probable* time of the next change in trend can be identified.

Figure 2-13 is a 5-year chart of Boatmans Bank. Twelve-week cycle lines have been fitted to the chart. Notice that the cycle lines correlate well with changes of trend. Cycle lines are another technique for targeting changes in trend. By themselves they can be erratic, and frequently not as precise as the ones illustrated in Figures 2-12 and 2-13; however, when used with Fourier analysis, their accuracy can be enhanced.

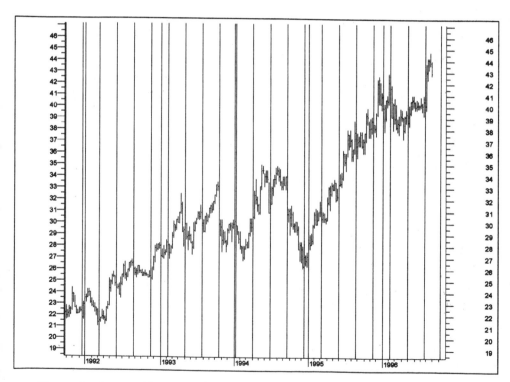

Figure 2-13   Weekly chart of Boatmans Bank stock with 12-week cycle lines plotted.

FOURIER ANALYSIS

Cycles can be found using a mathematical evaluation called Fourier analysis, available in the *Metastock* software package. It changes the price data into a set of sine waves representing major and minor cycles. When all the waves are combined, the result is the original data series. Almost any price series can be represented as a sine wave plus a series of harmonics. A harmonic is a sine wave that is a multiple of the fundamental sine wave, that is, a wave in which the cycles occur twice as often, or three times as often. For example, in the United States electrical power has a fundamental sine wave of 60 hertz (Hz), or 60 cycles per second (cps). Because of the way the power is generated there are also some harmonics included with the power. Mostly these are the third and fifth harmonics. That is to say, along with the 60-Hz component are components of 180 Hz and 300 Hz.

For example, a square wave can be expressed as a fundamental sine wave plus a series of odd harmonics.

Take the unlikely case of the square wave shown in Figure 2-14. The formula for a square wave reads as follows:

$$\text{Square wave } = \text{Sine}(wt) + 1/3 \text{ Sine}(3wt) + 1/5 \text{ Sine}(5wt)$$
$$+ 1/7 \text{ Sine}(7wt) + 1/9 \text{ Sine}(9wt) + 1/11 \text{ Sine}(11wt)$$
$$+ 1/13 \text{ Sine}(13wt)$$

and so forth.

This equation should be read: "Square wave is the fundamental sine wave plus one-third of the third harmonic plus one-fifth of the fifth harmonic plus one-seventh of the seventh harmonic plus one-ninth of the ninth harmonic plus one-eleventh of the eleventh harmonic plus one-thirteenth of the thirteenth harmonic . . . and so forth." Figure 2-14 shows how this works. Here we have only added the fundamental sine wave with one-third of the third harmonic, which are the first two terms of the previous equation. Notice how, with only this one harmonic added, the wave is closer to a square wave than a sine wave. Now imagine adding all the other odd harmonics. *Voila,* a square wave!

Any cyclic data can be separated into fundamental and multiple harmonic sine wave components. When this is done, the resulting equations can be used to target likely times when major and minor changes in trend can be expected.

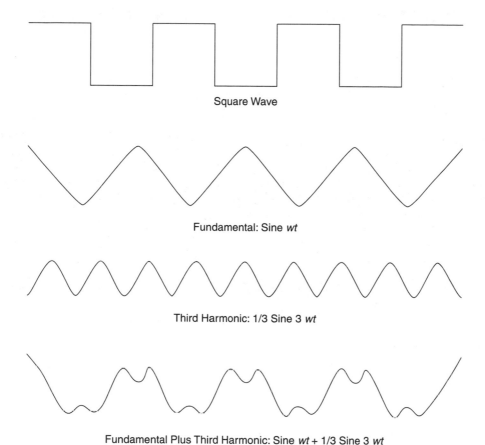

Square Wave

Fundamental: Sine *wt*

Third Harmonic: 1/3 Sine 3 *wt*

Fundamental Plus Third Harmonic: Sine *wt* + 1/3 Sine 3 *wt*

Figure 2-14 Development of a square wave from its fundamental and harmonic components.

Since the price movement of a stock tends to be cyclic, Fourier analysis can be applied to the historical data, and forecasts into the future can be made. Fourier analysis is a standard mathematical technique for finding cycles, and is sometimes called "spectral analysis."

Figure 2-15 is a daily bar chart of Augat with the results of a Fourier analysis shown below. This chart was made using the *Advanced G.E.T. 5.0*™ software package. This program combines analysis and forecasting by applying Fourier analysis to determine the sine-wave components of the price data, and then combining these cycles to show the probable point in time when trend changes might take place.

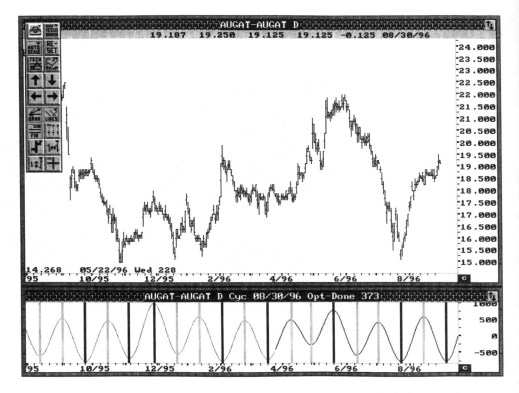

Figure 2-15   Changes in trend determined by Fourier analysis (see text).

The heavy black lines represent major changes in trend where multiple cycles or events coincide, and the lighter lines indicate minor changes in trend. This program uses an iterative approach to determining the cycles. In the example shown here, the number of iterations was 373,000, which took 20 minutes on a Pentium 90 computer.

The DOS and the Windows versions of *Metastock* include a feature that studies price movements by using Fourier analysis and indicates the three most dominant sine-wave components. Figure 2-16 shows the result of that analysis. In the top panel the Fourier analysis has identified the three sine-wave components with periods 51 days, 26 days, and 9 days.

Using the cycle program contained in both the DOS and Windows versions of *Metastock,* we can see whether these components have value. In the bottom panel of Figure 2-17 the cycle program plotted the first of these sine wave components, the 51-day cycle lines, and we can

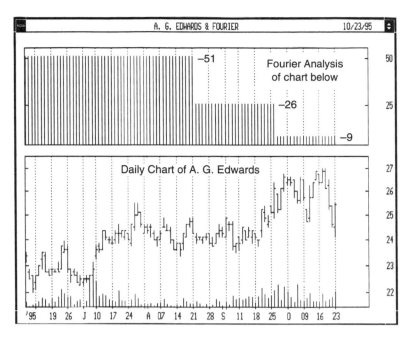

Figure 2-16   First three components of Fourier analysis of A. G. Edwards stock.

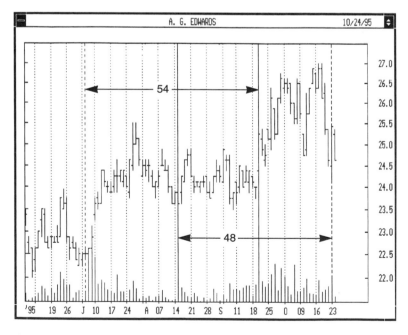

Figure 2-17   Conformation of 51-day cycle determined in Figure 2-16.

23

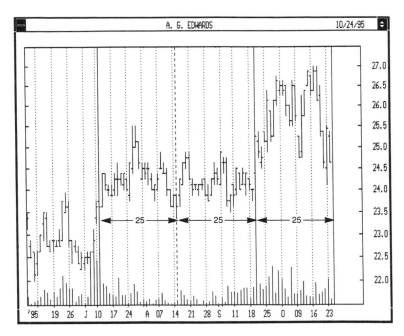

Figure 2-18 Conformation of 25-day cycle determined in Figure 2-16.

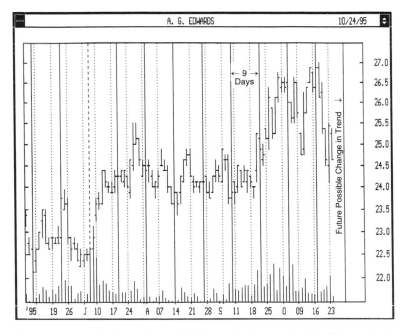

Figure 2-19 Conformation of 9-day cycle determined in Figure 2-16.

see that many of the changes in trend occur at the 54-day cycle, while changes in the down trend occur near the 48-day cycle for an average of 51 days. Twenty-five-day cycles are plotted in Figure 2-18. Again, many of the trend changes occur at or near the 25-day cycle. A 9-day cycle is plotted in Figure 2-19. Notice that many of the trend changes occur at or near the 9-day cycle points. Because of the effect of noise, this short day cycle is not as accurate as the 51- and 25-day cycles. Because changes in trend tend to occur at the cycle lines, lines can be extended into the future to pinpoint possible future changes in trend.

If the individual cycles represent methods of targeting probable changes in trend, then the points where these components coincide (come together) are more likely to identify points where trend changes might take place. In Figure 2-20 the 51- and 25-day cycles have been

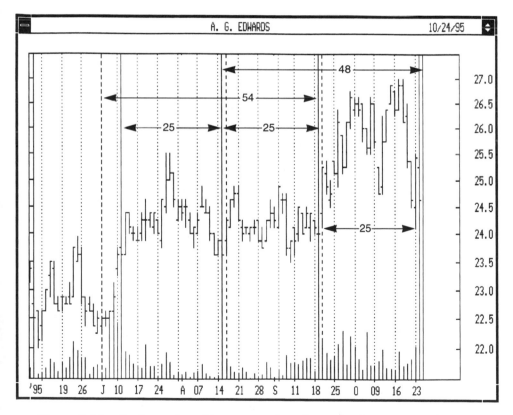

Figure 2-20 Conformation of how 51- and 25-day cycles line up to establish a possible time when a change of trend can occur.

plotted on the same graph. Notice that both cycles line up very closely around August 14 and September 18, 1995. When many lines cluster at the same point, it is a stronger signal that a change will take place at that point than is given by either line by itself.

GANN AND HIS ANGLES

William D. Gann, born in 1878 in Lufkin, Texas, was known as The Master Trader. His techniques helped to target the time when a change in trend might occur and the possible magnitude of that change. His methods have been used successfully for many years, and have increased in popularity in recent years.

The following appeared in the December 1909 issue of *Ticker Magazine* describing Gann's ability to forecast time and price targets:

> One of the most astonishing calculations made by Mr. Gann was during last summer [1909] when he predicted that September Wheat would sell at $1.20. This meant that it must touch that figure before the end of the month of September. At twelve o'clock, Chicago time, on September 30th (the last day) the option was selling below $1.08 and it looked as though his prediction would not be fulfilled. Mr. Gann said "If it does not touch $1.20 by the close of the market, it will prove that there is something wrong with my whole method of calculations. I do not care what the price is now, it must go there." It is common history that September Wheat surprised the whole country by selling at $1.20 and no higher in the last hour of trading, closing at that figure.

Gann believed in the existence of a natural order of everything in the universe. He was also very religious and often used biblical passages as a basis for his trading. The following passage from Ecclesiastes 1:9–10 was often quoted by Gann:

> What has been, that will be; what has been done, that will be done. Nothing is new under the sun. Even the thing of which we say, "See, this is new!" has already existed in the ages that preceded us."

Gann believed that this universal order of nature existed in the stock and commodity markets. Price movements were not random, but were predetermined. These predictable movements were the result of points of force found in nature. These forces of nature not only moved price, but could be predicted. For the most part, he relied on seasonality, which certainly satisfied his criteria.

Gann used a number of different methods to reach his predictions, not all of which were fully disclosed. Two of the disclosed methods, and those most widely used, are *Gann cyclic time analysis* and *Gann lines*. In Gann cyclic time analysis, a single fixed cycle is projected. In Figure 2-21, using only one pivot date, or anchor point, A, we choose to project a 30-day cycle, point B. Notice that this is the distance from the first low to the first high. The forecast change in trend is projected 30 days from point B, placing it at point C.

Gann had several cycles that he favored for his projections. Beginning with 91 days, he used a sequence of cycles 91, 182, 273, and 365 days which, of course, represents the calendar quarters associated with seasonality. Gann considered calendar periods very important and closely associated with the natural order.

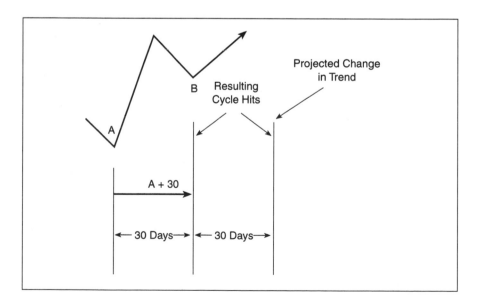

Figure 2-21 Projections of possible Gann cycles.

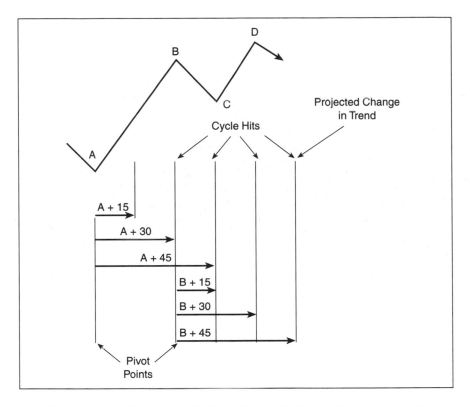

Figure 2-22   Multiple projection of possible Gann changes in trend.

Another form of Gann analysis projected several fixed cycles, as illustrated in Figure 2-22. Here we used cycles of 15, 30, and 45 days, projected from two pivot points, A and B, resulting in target points C, D, and E. In practice Gann used the following cycle periods, 30, 60, 91, 121, 152, 212, 243, 273, 304, 335, and 365 days. Because of the even division of the calendar year, Gann clearly put great store in natural cycles and their harmonics (in this case, subcycles).

In Figure 2-23 we have applied the technique demonstrated in Figure 2-22 to an actual security. Here the pivot points are marked with a "P," and the cycle periods were to Gann periods given above. The bars along the bottom of the chart show the number of cycle hits or clusters. Notice that changes of trend often take place at points where there are a large number of hits. Figure 2-24 illustrates the use of the data from Figure 2-23 to establish possible future turning points.

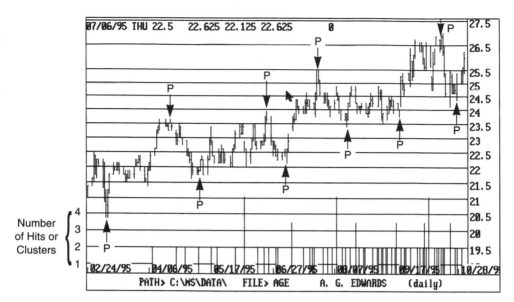

Figure 2-23 Automated multiple projections.

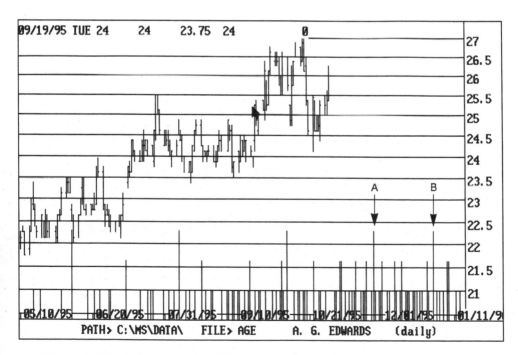

Figure 2-24 Using the data of Figure 2-23 to establish possible future turning points.

Gann believed that specific geometric patterns and angles had unique characteristics that could be used to predict price action. All of Gann's methods specify that equivalent time and price intervals be used on the chart so that a rise-to-run ratio of 1×1 appears as a 45 degree angle. Gann believed that prices could follow other angles that are related to the 1×1 ratio by integers. These ratios are 4×1, 2×1, 1×1, 1×2, 1×4. A set of these angles, called Gann fans, is shown in Figure 2-25. Notice that the price rise starts by following a 2×1 line, and after several weeks changes to follow the 1×1 line, and several months later switches to the 1×2 line.

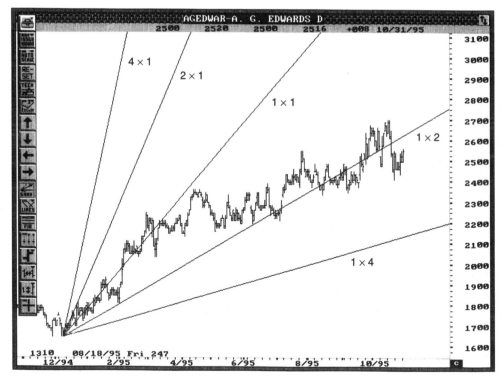

Figure 2-25   An example of Gann lines.

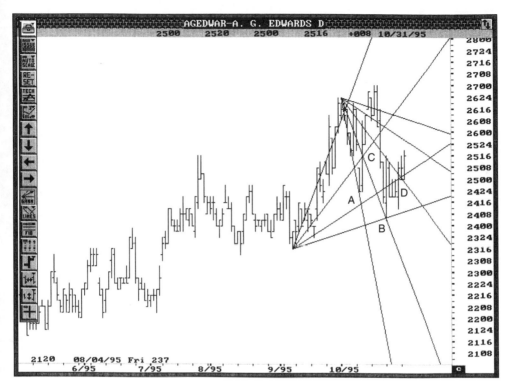

Figure 2-26 Example of using Gann lines to predict when a change of trend will occur.

Gann fans can be drawn from either the lows or highs of price movement. Gann also believed that the points where Gann lines intersect were where trend reversals would occur. In Figure 2-26 we have placed sets of Gann fans: one from a low point and one from a high point. Notice that trend reversals have taken place at point B. Also note that at points A and B the price action has been contained by the Gann lines.

3

TECHNICAL METHODS FOR SETTING TIME AND PRICE TARGETS

This chapter covers a variety of methods for setting time and price targets using support/resistance, channels of various types, and trendlines. Also, it discusses a number of moving averages, candlesticks, and other methods of plotting price movement that can confirm when a change of trend has taken place.

SUPPORT

Support can be defined as a price level of a commodity or stock at which buyers come into the market, thus forming a base that supports the price at that level. Support is a combination of psychological factors working upon the market participants, such as anticipation and general awareness of the possible development of a support level, plus external justification, such as economic factors, the cost of production, net worth (liquidated value), and so forth.

For example, if a stock goes up from $16.00 to $17.50, some potential purchasers will have missed getting in on the move. It is likely that

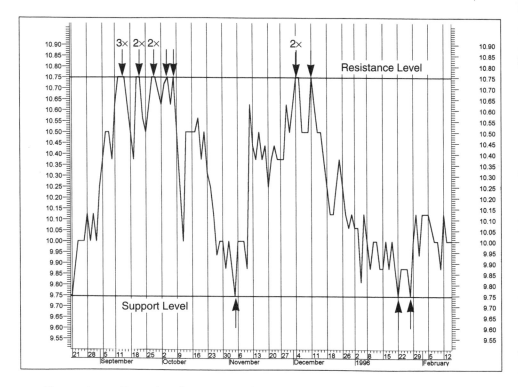

Figure 3-1 Example of support and resistance. Note that support line was "hit" four times and the resistance line was "hit" twelve times.

they are saying to themselves, "If that stock comes back to $16.00, I'll buy it." It is quite possible that some of them will actually enter resting buy orders for that level. Now this cluster of buy orders means that if the stock price comes down to $16.00, then the price cannot go below the $16.00 level until all the buy orders have been filled.

Figure 3-1 shows the support at $9.75, which existed for Sovereign Bank stock in the fall of 1995 and winter of 1996. Notice that the price fell to $9.75 in November, and then went back up. In January the price twice declined to $9.75, and then went up again. In essence, $9.75 acted as a floor, and as with any floor, if the floor fails, then a rapid descent may occur.

A support level can simply be the lowest price traded over an extended time period. Figure 3-2 is a chart of Helionetics stock, where

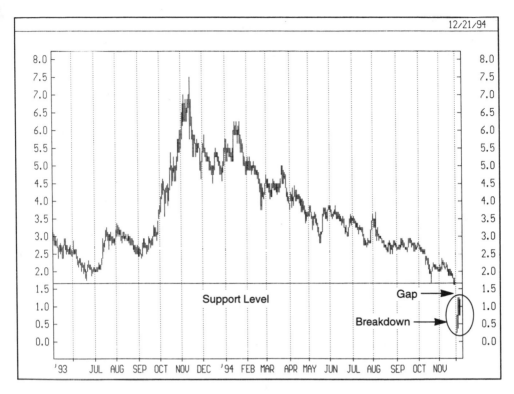

Figure 3-2   Here the support level and $1.75 was broken, which led to a major breakdown of the price, which reached $0.25, a loss of 83 percent.

support was found at about $1.62 in May–June 1993. When that level was breeched, the stock gapped down and traded as low as $0.25, a loss of 83 percent of its prior value. Subsequently the price returned to the $1.00 range, which represents a loss of 1/3 when compared to the support level of $1.62

RESISTANCE

Resistance can be defined as that price level at which sellers come into the market, halting the advance in price. Consider an investor who buys a stock or other security, and in a short time the stock goes up significantly. Now the investor is faced with a dilemma: Should he take his profits by selling the stock, or should he keep the stock with the hope that it will go higher. Many investors favor capturing substantial profits (say 10 or 15 percent within two weeks); therefore, the chances are great that profit taking will occur. There are many factors that cause prices to settle at low levels, but few that define a specific level that is *too* high.

In Figure 3-1 we see this phenomenon in action. The resistance level was at $10.75 and was tested 12 times in a period of 4 months. When a security is trading in the region between clearly defined support and resistance levels, as Sovereign Bank stock is doing in Figure 3-1, it is said that the stock is in a "trading range." As with support, breaking the resistance limit can yield some spectacular gains. The longer the security is in a trading range or "basing pattern," the more likely the breakout will be sensational.

Round numbers frequently act as resistance levels. The Dow Jones Industrial Average took three tries and many years to close above 1000. Each time it would approach this level and then retreat, only to take several years before trying again.

TRENDLINES

Trendlines are drawn from one extreme price to another along the tops or bottoms of a price chart. In a rising market, the trendline is drawn along the bottom of the prices, and in a falling market, it is drawn along the top of the prices. The longer a trend has been in force, and the more times the price touches the trendline without breaking it, the more significant the line becomes. A rising trendline is sometimes referred to as a *resistance line,* and a falling trendline is occasionally called a *supply line.* Trendlines exhibit the same characteristics as horizontal support and resistance. When broken, the lower support line, which defines an uptrend, frequently reverses to be a resistance line, while a falling line is often treated as support when penetrated.

Trendline A–A in Figure 3-3 was touched three times in 6 months. Note that after the trend was broken in late August, prices rallied to point C, where the line acted as resistance. After failing to breech that resistance, prices gapped downward the next day. Line B–B was formed from the highs in July and August and then tested four times,

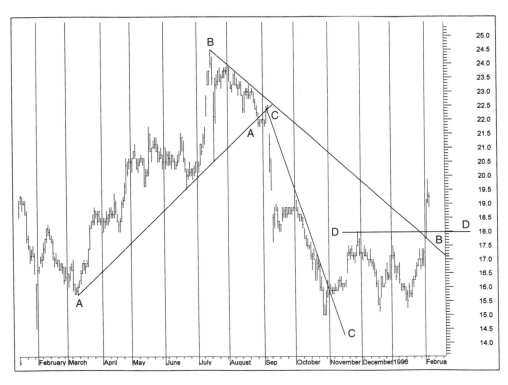

Figure 3-3 Examples of trendlines. Note the large losses that occurred with the breaking of trendline A-A. Also note the breakout to the upside when trendline B-B was breeched.

including point C. When the line was broken on February 1, the price jumped $1\frac{5}{8}$ points, or nearly 10 percent. Coming together with a new high for the previous three months, this breakout at B shows that traders act on price movement through the support and resistance lines. The breaking of line C–C in November marked the end of a sharp downward move and the beginning of a consolidation period.

CHANNELS

One of the oldest, and still one of the best ways to establish likely support and resistance levels, is by the use of channels. Methods for creating and finding channels are varied, and include, among others, parallel trendline channels, moving-average channels, Bollinger bands, and Raff channels.

Trend Channels

A trend channel can be created by drawing a line parallel to a trendline. An upwards trendline is traditionally drawn across two or more clear low prices and another line, parallel to the trendline, is drawn across the highest high. The chart of Advanced Micro Devices stock prices (Figure 3-4) illustrates this procedure. Notice that two different channels have been drawn, one long-term downtrend and one short-term uptrend. A close above the upper long-term channel line is considered to be a major bullish event, called an *upward breakout*.

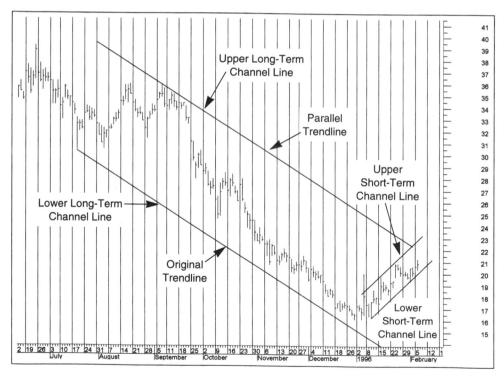

Figure 3-4   Channels created by drawing a line parallel to the trendline along the tops of the prices.

When the channel lines are clear to traders, they tend to contain the price movement, reversing whenever prices approach either the support or resistance levels channels. Trades can be initiated using the channel lines as a guide, selling when the price approaches the upper channel line and buying at the lower channel line. Therefore, the channel lines act as targets for both entering and exiting the trade. It is usually safe to enter trades in the direction of the trend.

Moving-Average Channels

Another way to create a channel is to use displaced moving averages. This is a pair of moving averages that have been moved either up or down, or left and right to form a channel. We use a simple moving average, which is the arithmetic average of the previous 10 days' price. For example, Figure 3-5 shows two 10-day moving averages of Circuit

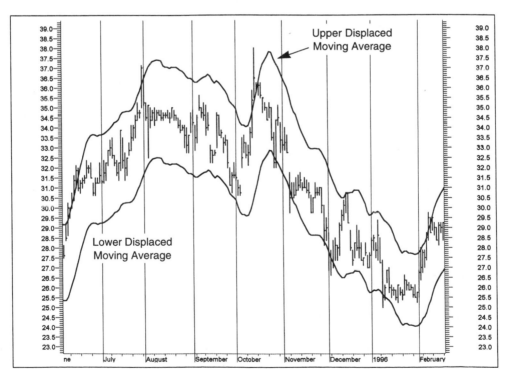

Figure 3-5　An example of channels being created by using displaced moving averages.

City stock. The top one is simply a 10-day moving average displaced 7 percent upwards, and the lower one is displaced –7 percent downwards. In the case of the upper band, there are only 3 days when prices *closed* above the band, and only two closes below the lower band. Traders use these bands just as they do straight-line trend channels, selling near the upper band and buying near the lower band.

Bollinger Bands

Bollinger bands are lines drawn at a distance of one or more standard deviations above and below a moving average. A *standard deviation* is a statistical term indicating the distribution of data with respect to a mean value. In this case, the mean value is the moving average. John Bollinger, the creator of the bands, recommends using a 20-unit moving average and a standard deviation of 2.0; however, it is common to find traders using a 10-day moving average and a standard deviation of 1.5.

Figure 3-6 is a plot of Homestead Mines stock price with a 20-day moving average of the close, and upper and lower bands located 2.0 standard deviations from the moving average. Notice that almost all the prices are contained by the bands. Observe that the distance between the upper and lower bands is constantly changing. This distance is a measure of volatility. When there is little price movement, the bands tend to come closer together, and when the price is moving upwards or downwards rapidly, the bands grow further apart. A popular strategy is to buy when the price of the security is near the lower band, and sell when it is near the top band.

Raff Channels

Linear regression analysis, sometimes called *least-squares analysis,* can be thought of as a way of determining the best straight line through a series of data points. The least-squares method finds a straight line through prices that minimizes the distances between the prices and the closest point on the resulting trendline.

Raff channels (created by Gilbert Raff) are lines drawn parallel to a linear regression line, one drawn above the prices and the other

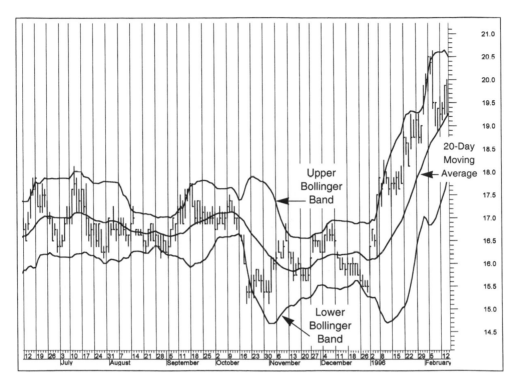

Figure 3-6 An example of channels being created by using Bollinger bands. These channels are named after John Bollinger, who first described them.

below. The lines are spaced an equal distance from the linear regression line. The parallel lines are located such that one, but possibly both lines touch the most extreme price excursion from the trendline. Figure 3-7 is a weekly plot of the OEX, with the regression line and Raff channel lines plotted on the data. Note that the lines are equally spaced, and the spacing was determined by the relative low price in mid-January 1996.

Figure 3-8 is a daily chart of the OEX, where the major Raff channel has been plotted showing the overall trend. In addition, six minor Raff channels have been plotted, illustrating the short-term trends that existed within the major trend. As with other channels, Raff regression channels can be traded by buying when the price is near the lower channel and selling when the price is near the upper channel.

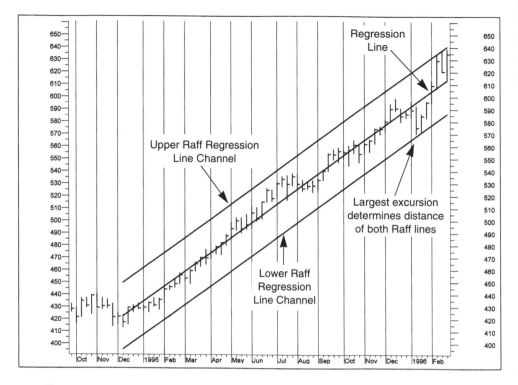

Figure 3-7 This is another way of creating a channel. In this case, a regression line has been created, and two lines touching the tops and bottoms of the price action have been drawn parallel to the regression line. Channels created in this way are called Raff regression channels, after the man who created them.

Buying when the price is near the lower channel and selling when the price is near the upper channel is an excellent tactic; however, confirmation by some other indicator would improve the results considerably. In all security analysis, both fundamental and technical, the confirming of one method with another greatly increases the likelihood the correct analysis has been made. Triple or quadruple confirmations strengthen the analysis still further. The balance of this chapter and the next chapter present an overview of the variety of techniques that can be used to gain confirmation.

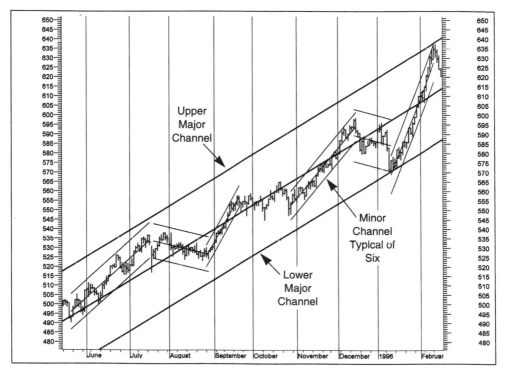

Figure 3-8   Here we have plotted both long-term Raff channels, but also a number of short-term Raff channels.

MOVING AVERAGES

One of the simplest indicators is the moving average. The most basic trading method is to buy when the price of a security is above the moving average, and sell when it goes below the moving average. Popular time periods for the moving average calculations for this purpose are 200, 50, and 20 days, depending on the time horizon.

Figure 3-9 is a *weekly* plot of Anheuser-Busch from early 1991. Superimposed on the price data is a 40-week (200-day) moving average. If you bought whenever the price of the stock was above the moving average, and sold when below, you would have been mostly in the market

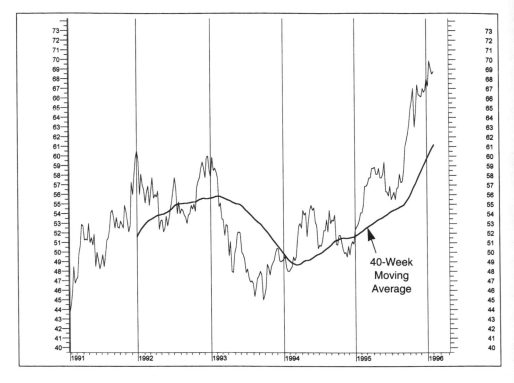

Figure 3-9   Weekly plot of Anheuser-Busch stock with a 40-week (200-day) moving average superimposed.

when the stock was going up and out when it was going down. The trends identified by this technique are clear, and there are only a few cases where prices flounder and the trend signal is wrong.

Figure 3-10 is a *daily* chart of Anheuser-Busch with a 50-day moving average. As expected, the trades are shorter, more trades are created, and naturally there are more whipsaws, that is, trades where no profits are made.

Displaced Moving Averages

Figure 3-11 is a weekly plot of AT&T with a 40-week moving average. If we had followed the "buy when above and sell when below" strategy, we would have been badly whipsawed in late 1991–early 1992, and

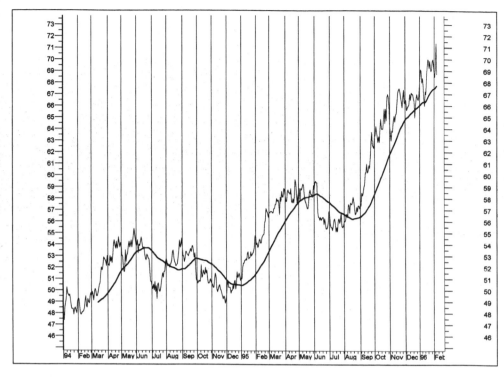

Figure 3-10   Daily plot of Anheuser-Busch stock with a 50-day moving average superimposed.

again in the period between mid-1994 and mid-1995. Figure 3-12 is exactly the same, except the moving average has been displaced 14 weeks to the right. Now there are only a few whipsaws. The price that was paid for eliminating so many whipsaws is that the exit in 1993 is delayed, with some loss of profit.

Dual Moving Averages

A popular moving average system is the dual moving-average system. Here we utilize the crossing of a short-term and a long-term moving average. The strategy is to buy when the shorter moving average goes above the longer-term moving average, and sell when the shorter moving average goes below the long-term moving average. Although a number of averages have been suggested, the 4–18 or 5–20 pairs seem to be the most popular.

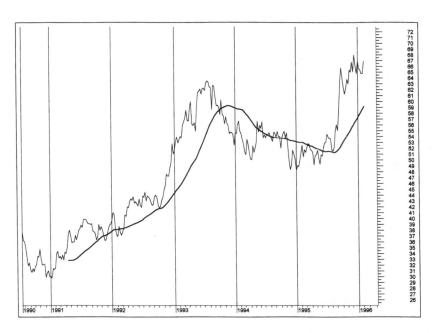

Figure 3-11 Weekly chart of AT&T with 40-week moving average superimposed. Note that if trades had been initiated on the crossing of the moving average, a lot of whipsaws would have been created. Compare to Figure 3-12.

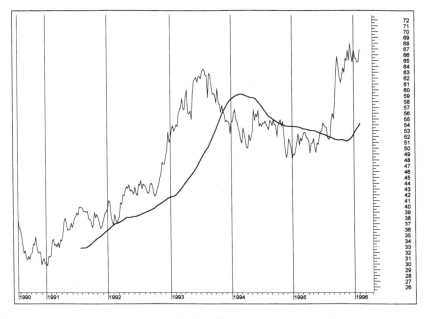

Figure 3-12 This chart is identical to Figure 3-10, except the moving average has been moved 14 weeks to the right. Note the large reduction in whipsaws.

Figure 3-13 shows a chart of Cracker Barrel stock with 5-week and 20-week moving averages superimposed on the chart. The prices have been shown as close prices rather than the customary high, low, close bars. This was done so that the movements of the moving averages could be easily seen. Above the price chart is a plot of the price oscillator. The price oscillator displays the difference between the two moving averages of the security's price. If the price oscillator is above zero, then the 5-week moving average has crossed above the 20-week moving average. Thus, if the price oscillator crosses above "zero," a buy signal is generated. Alternately, a cross below "zero" generates a sell signal. It is sometimes hard to see the crossings of the two moving averages

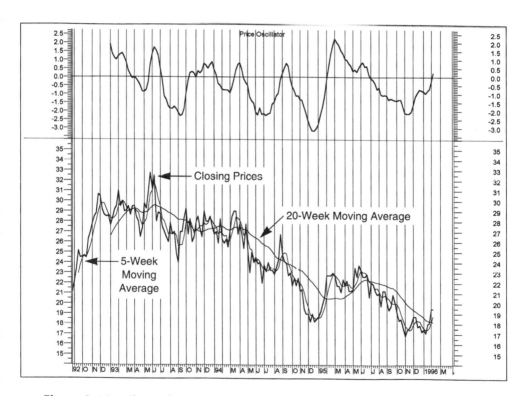

Figure 3-13 Chart of Cracker Barrel stock with 5- and 20-week moving averages superimposed. The upper window is a price oscillator, which is calculated by subtracting the 5-week moving average from the 20-week moving average. Note that the price oscillator crosses zero when the 5-week moving average crosses the 20-week moving average.

when plotted on a price chart, whereas the "zero" crossings of the price oscillator are easily seen. Most technical-analysis packages contain software for plotting the price oscillator.

Most of the charts shown in this book are in an upward or bullish trend. In this case the stock was definitely in a downward or bearish trend. Notice that the dual moving average, while not making a profit, did, however, keep an investor out of the stock during most of the major downturns.

CANDLESTICKS

Candlesticks were invented by the Japanese hundreds of years ago as a way of studying the price activity of rice. The top and bottom of the wick represents the high and low of the day. The top and bottom of the body represent either the open or close, depending on whether the close was above or below the open. The color of the body shows whether the price ended up or down. Traditionally, up closes are red and down closes are black. However, for the purpose of this book, we will use white and black. Figure 3-14 shows the two types of candlesticks and labels the component parts.

Figure 3-15 is a plot using candlesticks. Compare it to some of the other plots that used conventional high, low, and close bar charts. Can

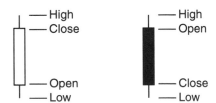

Figure 3-14   Examples of up-day and down-day candlesticks. The white-bodied candlestick represents an up day, that is, the close was higher than the open, and the black bodied represents a down day, that is, the close was lower than the open.

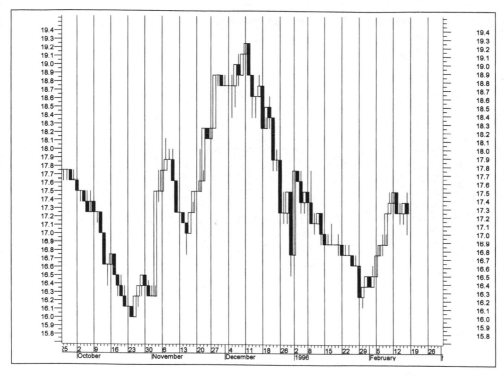

Figure 3-15 Chart using candlesticks. Compare to conventional bar charts.

you locate some of the patterns shown in Figures 3-16 and 3-17 in this graph?

Over the years certain patterns have come to be recognized as bullish or bearish. Figures 3-16 and 3-17 show some of the bearish patterns, while Figures 3-18 and 3-19 show the bullish patterns. Most technical-analysis programs have the ability to plot candlestick patterns. If the close is not available, some programs use the previous close as the open price. The reader is cautioned that such patterns may not be accurate because of gaps and other phenomena. Some traders are very high on candlesticks and others find them mysterious. Each reader must put his own valuation on candlesticks.

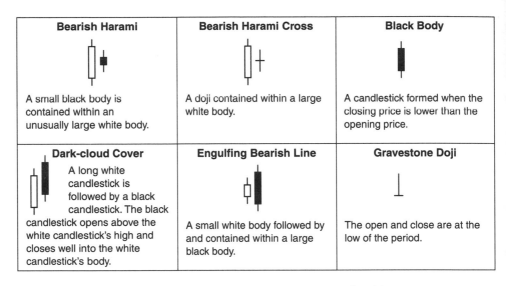

Figure 3-16   A collection of bearish candlesticks.

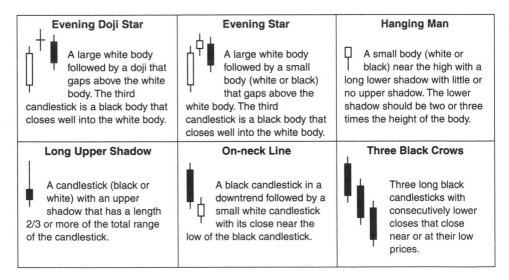

Figure 3-17   More bearish candlesticks.

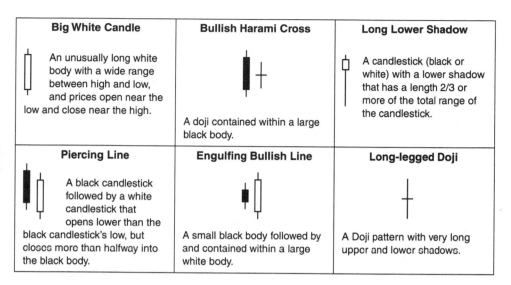

Big White Candle	Bullish Harami Cross	Long Lower Shadow
An unusually long white body with a wide range between high and low, and prices open near the low and close near the high.	A doji contained within a large black body.	A candlestick (black or white) with a lower shadow that has a length 2/3 or more of the total range of the candlestick.
Piercing Line	Engulfing Bullish Line	Long-legged Doji
A black candlestick followed by a white candlestick that opens lower than the black candlestick's low, but closes more than halfway into the black body.	A small black body followed by and contained within a large white body.	A Doji pattern with very long upper and lower shadows.

Figure 3-18   A collection of bullish candlesticks.

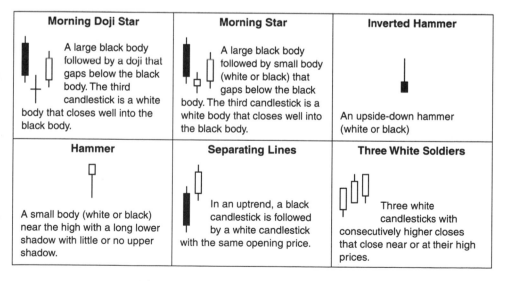

Morning Doji Star	Morning Star	Inverted Hammer
A large black body followed by a doji that gaps below the black body. The third candlestick is a white body that closes well into the black body.	A large black body followed by small body (white or black) that gaps below the black body. The third candlestick is a white body that closes well into the black body.	An upside-down hammer (white or black)
Hammer	Separating Lines	Three White Soldiers
A small body (white or black) near the high with a long lower shadow with little or no upper shadow.	In an uptrend, a black candlestick is followed by a white candlestick with the same opening price.	Three white candlesticks with consecutively higher closes that close near or at their high prices.

Figure 3-19   More bullish candlesticks.

POINT-AND-FIGURE CHARTS

Point-and-figure charts have been in use for over 100 years, and can be said to have passed the test of time. Point-and-figure charts, because of their simplicity, can be very valuable to the user. Like moving averages they filter out static and minor price movements. Because point-and-figure charts exclude static, and the time scale, they allow the technician to focus on pure price movement.

Point-and-figure charts are made up of columns of Xs and Os. The Xs represent advancing prices and the Os declining prices. There is no time scale, and each column can represent any length of time.

When setting up a point-and-figure chart, box size and reversal units must be chosen. Box size refers to how many price units are represented by each box. The reversal units allude to the number of boxes used to establish when a column of Os reverses to a column of Xs. Figure 3-20 illustrates 10-point boxes with 3-box reversal. Three-box reversal is used almost universally, although other numbers can be used.

In Figure 3-20 a value of 115 would not cause another X to be plotted, whereas a value of 120 would be. A value of 90 would not cause a new column of Os to be generated since a value of 80 is required. That is to say, values between 81 and 119 do not cause any action on the part of the plotter.

Box and reversal size determine the sensitivity of the chart. Figure 3-21 is a point-and-figure chart using a box size of 1 and a reversal value of 3. The same information plotted using a box size of 0.33 and reversal value of 2 is shown in Figure 3-22. Note that the second chart is much more detailed. Also, on the second chart a trendline A–A has been drawn, and the violation of that trendline signaled the start of a new up trend.

OTHER METHODS OF PLOTTING PRICE ACTION
(RENKE, KAGI, AND THREE-LINE BREAK)

Steve Nison, a well-known authority on candlestick charting, has also written about other Japanese methods of plotting price action, such as Kagi, three-line break, and Renko. The use of these techniques is beyond the scope of this book, but the reader should be aware that there are other techniques beyond bar, candlesticks, and point-and-figure

```
130
120                          X      Need 120 or higher to plot
                                    another X going up
110    X             X    O    X
100    X    O        X    O    X
 90    X    O        X    O    X
 80    X    O        X    O    X
 70    X    O             O    X
 60         O                       Need 80 or lower to reverse and plot
                                    three Os going down
```

10-Point Boxes with 3-Box Reversal

Figure 3-20   Example of a point-and-figure plot.

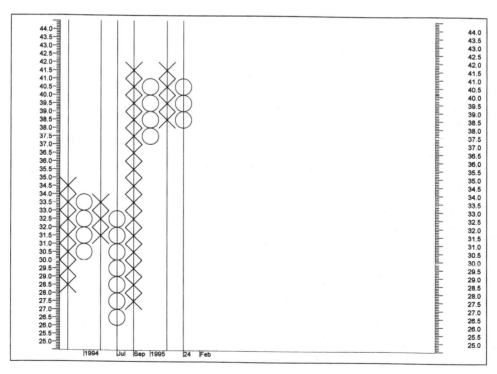

Figure 3-21   Example of a point-and-figure plot using a box size of 1 and a reversal value of 3. Compare to Figure 3-22, which uses different values.

53

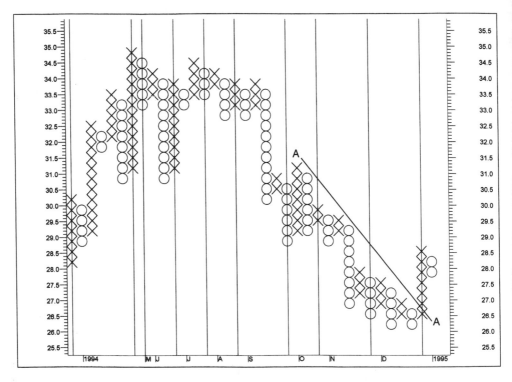

Figure 3-22   Example of a point-and-figure plot using a box size of 0.33 and a reversal value of 2. Compare to Figure 3-21. Note that a trendline has been drawn on the chart in the same fashion that trendlines are drawn on conventional bar or candlestick charts.

charts. The reader is directed to Steven Nison's text, *Beyond Candlesticks* (John Wiley, New York, 1994). These plotting techniques are becoming available in the more popular computer technical-analysis programs.

ELLIOTT WAVES

To the uninformed, a chart of the stock or commodity markets looks chaotic, or at best as though it has no discernible patterns.

In 1934 Ralph Nelson Elliott, an accountant by profession, formulated a theory concerning the natural laws that govern all of man's activities, including the financial markets.

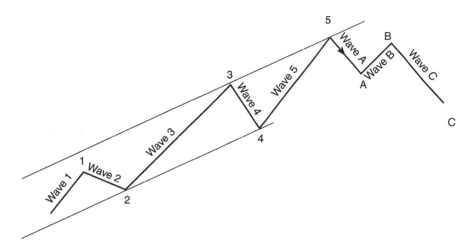

Figure 3-23 Idealized Elliott wave.

Figure 3-23 is an idealized Elliott wave. Note that the upwards section is composed of five waves: three up and two down. These are usually numbered as shown. Note that the downward portion is three waves long—two down and one up—and is customarily labeled with a letter for identification.

As might be expected from previous discussions, it is crowd psychology that causes the Elliott wave to take the shape it does. A few people know of an event that they believe will drive a particular security higher, and as a result, they buy. A little later, the security has gone up in price (wave 1), so they sell and take their profit. Naturally, other people have observed the price movement and thought, "This security is a mover, and if the price comes back down to X, I'll buy." Maybe they even enter orders at X dollars. When the first group takes their profit, the price falls (wave 2). When it reaches X dollars, the buy orders are activated and other orders are entered, and the price begins to climb (wave 3); others notice the price action and they buy, forcing the price still higher. Eventually, the price climbs so high that profit taking sets in, and the price begins to fall (wave 4). However, based on the previous price action, there are buyers who are waiting for the price to fall enough that they can activate buy orders. When this happens, the new buyers (or old buyers who got out with a profit) begin to drive the price back up (wave 5). Eventually, the price goes so high that a large number of people begin to sell in order to lock in their profit, and the price falls (wave A). When the price falls sufficiently, a new crowd is attracted to the security, although a fewer number than previously and the price goes up some (wave B). When this group and others take their profit, the price falls again (wave C), and now things are ready to start all over again.

Each wave in turn may be broken down into Elliott-wave components, and these in turn may consist of Elliott-wave components. For example, wave 1 may consist of a five-wave numbered series and wave 2 by a three-wave lettered sequence. Figure 3-24, two months of the price movement on Xerox, is an example of Elliott-wave analysis applied to stock prices. Note that wave 3 is broken down to a five-wave sequence.

Figure 3-24   Elliott-wave analysis applied to Xerox stock prices. Note the fifth wave failure, which causes the development of a double top, a very bearish formation.

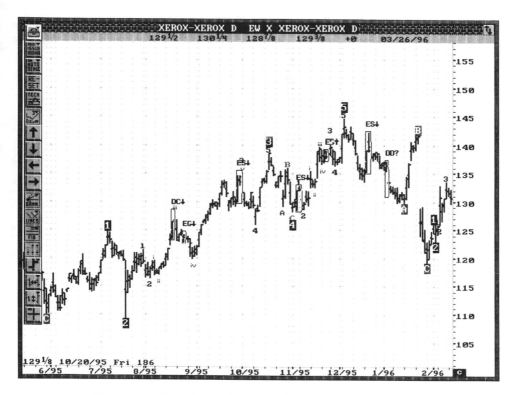

Figure 3-25 A long time view of Xerox stock. Note, for example, that leg three is composed of five waves, some of which in turn are divided into five waves. Also note the A–B–C consolidation waves after the fifth wave. This is an excellent example of Elliott-wave theory.

Figure 3-25, a longer-term plot of Xerox, shows the full cycle of five waves up, and three down, with many of the waves broken down into smaller waves. Note that wave 3 is broken down into five waves, indicated by the small numbers, and that the third wave of this minor wave is in turn broken down into five waves, labeled with Roman numerals. Note that the A wave, although not labeled, consists of another three-wave series.

The five-wave series can be applied to downward trends as well as to upward trends. Figure 3-26 shows how a downward trend would be labeled. Here again some of the waves are broken down into more waves, which are broken down still further.

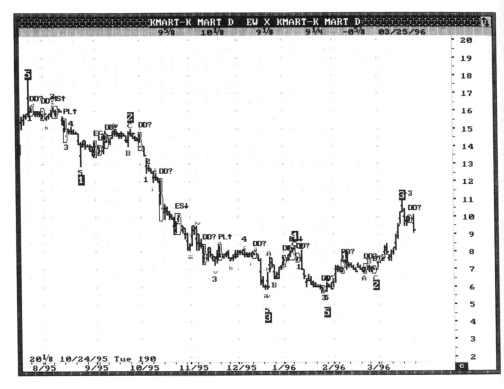

Figure 3-26   Elliott-wave theory can be applied to downward trends as well as to up trends.

Elliott waves can be applied to any time frame, and are useful for day trading, as well as analyzing long-term trends using yearly charts. Figure 3-27 is a long-term weekly chart of Xerox showing the five-wave sequence. Notice that the sequence shown in Figure 3-25 now occupies a small part of the chart, and that the wave count is so minor compared to the overall chart that it is labeled with Roman numerals. When doing Elliott analysis, as with other technical analysis, it is prudent to look at both the long-term and short-term periods.

Figures 3-24 through 3-29 were made using software that labels the waves automatically. The value of Elliott waves is that they inform the analyst of both where the price of the security is in the long-term cycle, and the direction prices are likely to follow. One of the early prob-

Figure 3-27 Weekly chart of Xerox. Note the information shown in Figure 3-25 occupies only a small section of this chart. This shows that Elliott waves can be applied in all time frames.

lems with Elliott-wave analysis was that not everyone counted the waves the same way. However, with the advent of software programs that mechanically count the waves, this subjectiveness should become a thing of the past.

One way to trade using the Elliott wave is to identify the fourth wave, and using a trendline or displaced moving average, buying when it is violated. An example is shown in Figure 3-28, where the stock is in a fourth wave. A trendline has been added. The next day is shown in Figure 3-29, and the trendline has been significantly broken, indicating a buy signal. Examining Figure 3-25 reveals that the price advanced $10 in the subsequent three weeks.

Figure 3-28   Illustration of how adding a trendline to a wave-4 formation can be used to trade. See Figure 3-29, which shows the breakout forming the start of wave 5.

There are a few rules that apply to Elliott-wave analysis:

1. Wave 2 must never go below the starting price for wave 1.
2. Wave 4 should never go below the top of wave 1.
3. In a security whose price is moving rapidly upwards, the A–B–C correction may trend upwards rather than down, as is normal.
4. Wave 5 does not necessarily have to go higher than wave 3. This is how double tops are formed, and is referred to as a "failed fifth wave."

The wave series shown in Figure 3-24 is an example of fifth-wave failure. Usually, the height of waves 3 and 5 have a Fibonacci relation-

Figure 3-29　Shows the breakout from wave 4 to a wave 5.

ship to wave 1. Because of this relationship, it becomes possible to target points where the waves will end. (Fibonacci numbers are covered in detail in Chapter 6.) Figure 3-30 is a monthly chart presenting the information contained in Figure 3-27, to which Fibonacci accordions have been added. The first accordion A–A was placed around wave 1. Notice that projection 2 is within one point of the ultimate height of wave 5. A second pair B–B was placed around wave 1 of wave 3, and its Fibonacci number, 2.62, just happens to line up with the end of wave 5. Another pair C–C was placed around the data of wave 5 of wave 3, and again its Fibonacci number, 1.38, came exactly at the top of wave 5. Here, using data from 1991, 1992, and 1994, Fibonacci sequences were used to predict the probable top for this stock. The fact that all three lined up, which no other pairs of Fibonacci numbers did, is a powerful predictor of the probable top. The fact that the level of a probable 1995 top was

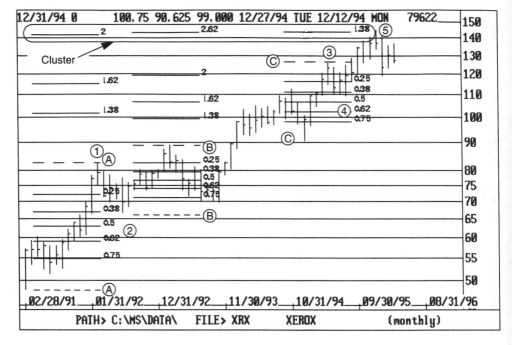

Figure 3-30   Application of Fibonacci calipers. See text for details.

predicted back in 1991 illustrates the power of Fibonacci numbers when applied to the security markets. Skilled users of the Elliott-wave/ Fibonacci combination set sell orders at the predicted top, thus maximizing their profit.

Although in this case the height of wave 1 equaled the height of waves 2, 3, 4, and 5 combined, it is normal for wave 3 to be the longest, and wave 5 to be shorter but longer than wave 1. The wavelength relationships shown in Figure 3-23 are more common than those shown in the Xerox example.

4

OSCILLATORS

Although channels are a good way of trading, they can be improved by obtaining confirmation from other sources. A group of indicators that can confirm the channels are called *oscillators*.

Many people have studied the securities markets with the hope of inventing a perfect oscillator, and there are probably at least 100 oscillators appearing somewhere in the literature; none of them perfect, but some of them quite useful. They vary from "A," the Accumulation Swing Index, to "U," the ultimate oscillator. Here we deal with the ones that have stood the test of time and proven useful in actual practice.

MOVING AVERAGE CONVERGENCE DIVERGENCE OSCILLATOR (MACD)

In 1979 Gerald Appel improved the price oscillator, discussed in Chapter 3, by adding a moving average of the price oscillator itself. Buy signals came when the price oscillator moved above the second moving average, called a *trigger line*. He called the new technical oscillator the *Moving Average Convergence Divergence Oscillator,* or MACD (pronounced M-A-C-D, or Mac-D). Buy signals are generated when the price oscillator goes above the trigger line, and sell signals come when the price oscillator falls below the trigger line.

Figure 4-1 shows the addition of the trigger line to the price oscillator that was first plotted in Figure 3-13. The two combined oscillators make up the MACD. Note that this MACD is much faster to signal entrances into upward trends and also much quicker to get out of losing trades. Prove this for yourself by comparing Figures 3-13 and 4-1.

Appel studied the MACD at great length and has made a series of recommendations, some of which can be summarized as follows:

1. Establish the trend of the security by determining whether the 50-unit moving average has a positive or negative slope. If positive, use a fast MACD to get into the trade; if negative, use a slow MACD to get into the trade.

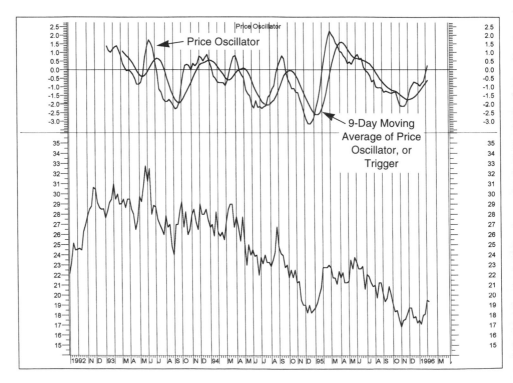

Figure 4-1 Price oscillator with a 9-day moving average added to become a MACD.

2. The parameters for a fast MACD buy would be to use 6–19 units for the price-oscillator portion and a 6-unit trigger.

3. The parameters for a slow MACD buy would be to use 13–26 units for the dual moving-average portion and a 9-unit trigger.

4. The sell signal for either the fast or slow MACD entry would be a 19–39-unit dual moving average and a 9-unit trigger.

5. Divergences (discussed in the next section of this chapter) between the MACD and the price of the security increases the strength of the buy or sell signals.

6. Once a sell signal has occurred, the trade should not be reentered until the MACD has returned to below "zero," even if a buy signal is received.

DIVERGENCES

A divergence occurs when an oscillator is rising while the security's price is making a new low. Alternatively, a divergence occurs when the security's price is making a new high, but the oscillator is not making a new high.

Figure 4-2 illustrates this point exceedingly well. Line A–A shows a rise in the price of Novell stock. Line B–B shows that, while prices are making new highs, the MACD is failing to make new highs; that is, a divergence is occurring. This means that the sell signal at point C is very important. Note that shortly after the C sell signal, the price gapped down, and in a matter of a few days the price fell nearly 25 percent. Lines D–D and F–F are divergent. Prices are making new lows, but the MACD is not. Here, after the buy signal given at point F, the stock rallied nearly 20 percent. There are more divergences in the chart, which were not identified, but signaled major price moves. Can you locate one or more?

Divergent analysis is applicable to nearly all oscillators. Figure 4-3 shows three very different oscillators: momentum, Trix, and Relative Strength Index, all of which exhibited divergences similar to the one illustrated in Figure 4-2.

The underlying cause of divergences can be explained as follows. When a stock (or other security) first begins to move, people who have been watching the price action of the stock note that the price is moving up and buy, causing still more movement attracting still more

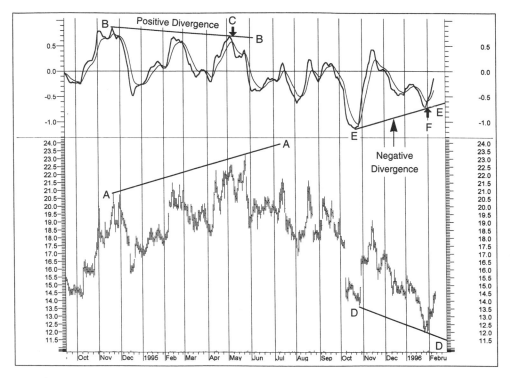

Figure 4-2 Examples of divergences, both at a market top and a market bottom.

buyers, who in turn attract still more buyers, causing still higher prices. Eventually, prices go high enough that early buyers begin to take profits, thereby halting the advance or even causing prices to retreat. Line A–A in Figure 4-4 illustrates this scenario.

Prices now pull back sufficiently to attract new buyers, and possibly some of the old buyers who sold near the top. What is different about this advance is there are fewer buyers than during the first advance, which makes the runup of prices less dramatic. This price runup is shown by line B–B. Note that the slope of line B–B is not as steep as that of line A–A because of the reduced demand. This difference is recognized by the oscillator (in this case the MACD) by the slopes of lines AI–AI and BI–BI. The lower slope of line BI–BI over a similar time span means that the second oscillator peak never has the chance to get as high as the previous peak. The lines C–C, CI–CI and D–D, DI–DI illustrate the same mechanisms at work when the price is declining.

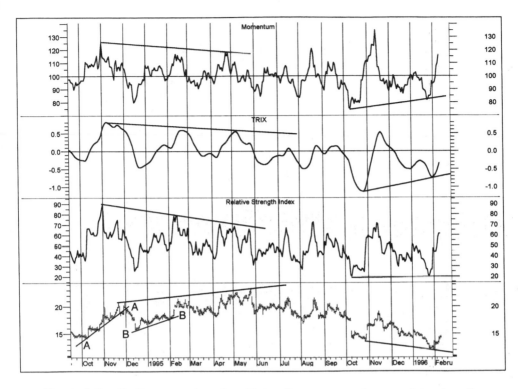

Figure 4-3 Further examples of oscillator divergences using a variety of oscillators.

Technical-analysis using oscillators, combined with divergence analysis, can be one of the most powerful tools available for determining probable future price action. A strong divergence usually means that the price action is about to reverse, signaling that appropriate action should be taken. Some of the possible oscillators available for this type of analysis are covered in the next few sections of this chapter.

RELATIVE STRENGTH INDEX

The Relative Strength Index (RSI) was first introduced by J. Welles Wilder in June 1978 in *Commodities Magazine*. The name Relative Strength Index is misleading, because the index compares the internal strength of a single security—*not* the strength of one security—to an-

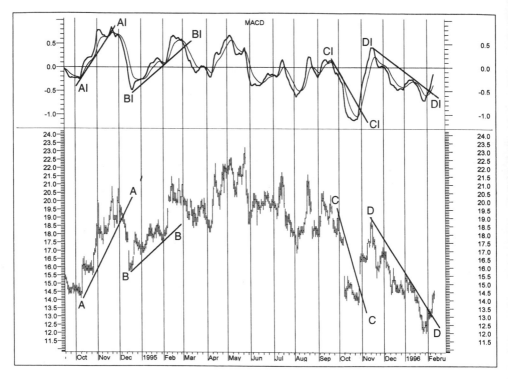

Figure 4-4 Chart showing the underlying cause of divergences. See text for explanation.

other, or a security to an index. Equis International in their manual for the Metastock program states that a more appropriate name might be *Internal Strength Index*.

When Wilder first introduced the RSI, he recommended using a 14-day period in the calculations. Since then much research has been done on this indicator by Andrew Cardwell, who recommends calculations based on a 12-day period. He suggests several ways of trading the RSI.

The first is to plot a 45-day moving average of the RSI, buying when the RSI goes above the moving average and selling when it goes below. This technique is illustrated in Figure 4-5. This method does an excellent job of staying with the trend and results in timely exits; however, it tends to generate a lot of whipsaws during consolidation phases.

The second method involves drawing trendlines on the RSI, then buying or selling when the trendline is crossed. In Figure 4-6, trend

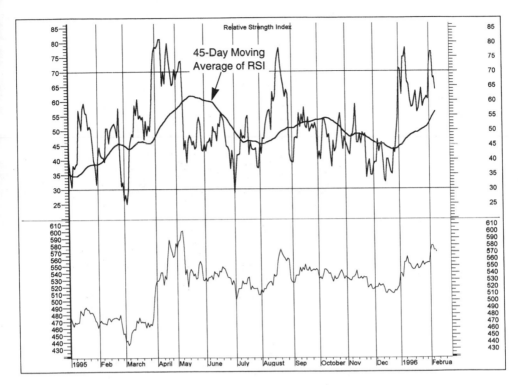

Figure 4-5   Relative Strength Index with a 45-day moving average.

A–A on the RSI is broken before trend B–B on the price chart. Using the RSI-trend violation, rather than the price-trend violation, would generate more profit retention. The same is true of trends C–C and D-D. Trends E–E and F–F illustrate using this technique to affect entries. In this case, the breaking of trend E–E causes earlier entry than does the breaking of F–F. Although this technique provides excellent exit and entry points, it is probably best used in cooperation with another indicator, such as the MACD or stochastic.

ON-BALANCE VOLUME

In general, volume indicators do not work very well; however, the on-balance volume indicator (OBV) is the exception. Joe Grandville is the father of on-balance volume. OBV is calculated by determining whether

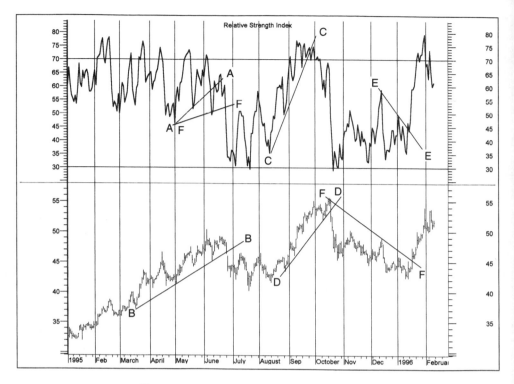

Figure 4-6   Trendlines drawn on the RSI.

today's close is greater than yesterday's. If so, then today's volume is added to yesterday's OBV. If not, then today's volume is subtracted from yesterday's OBV.

Several methods of trading the OBV have been developed. The first uses trendlines on the OBV, combined with divergence analysis, buying or selling when the trendline is broken. The second uses a moving average of the OBV. A popular period for the moving average is 39. Buys are initiated when the OBV is above the moving average. Figure 4-7 shows both of these methods. Lines A–A and B–B are trendlines drawn on the OBV, and the smooth line is the 39-unit moving average. Neither of these methods resulted in optimum entries and exits, but they both stayed with the trends. The moving-average technique was subject to whipsaws during consolidation periods.

It is probably best if the OBV is used as a confirming indicator for other indicators, such as the MACD, or, alternatively, used as a primary

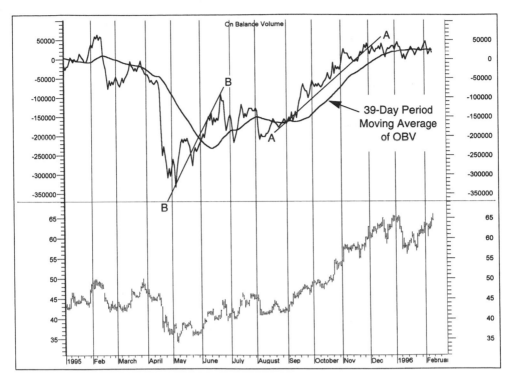

Figure 4-7 On-balance volume with 39-day moving average and trendlines.

indicator using the stochastic (discussed in the next section) or MACD indicators as confirming indicators. People working with Neural Networks report excellent results using the OBV as one of the inputs.

STOCHASTIC OSCILLATOR

The *stochastic* oscillator measures where today's price is relative to the range of prices over the last X number of days. For example, if the range of prices over the last 14 days was from 350 to 360, and today's price was 355, then the stochastic would be 50 percent. Said another way, the range was 10 (360–350) and today's price within the range was 5 (355–350), so 5 (today's price) divided by 10 (the range) multiplied by 100 to convert to percent, yields the stochastic, or as it is termed, %K. This value is called the *raw %K* and is very volatile.

It is customary to smooth this value with a moving average. Values used for smoothing are usually in the range between 3 and 5. The smoothed stochastic is called the *smoothed %K*. It is normal to add a moving average to the smoothed %K to act as a trigger similar to the trigger of the MACD. The most common values for the %K is in the 5–20 range, with 5 and 14 being very common values. Trigger values usually fall in the 3–5 range.

The top graph of Figure 4-8 shows the raw %K, while the middle graph depicts the smoothed %K with a five-period moving average. The trigger in both cases was a five-period moving average. The bottom graph is a bar graph of the Boeing Company.

There are three ways to trade the stochastic oscillator:

1. Buy when the oscillator (either %K or divergence (%D)) falls below a specific level (for example, 20), and then rises above

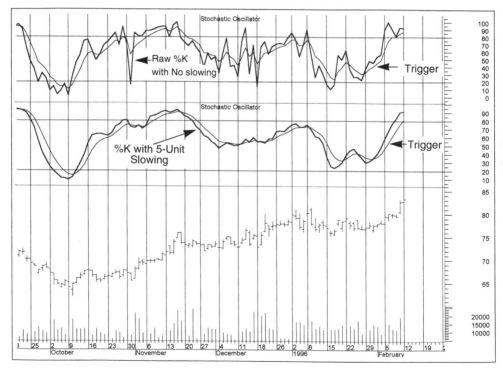

Figure 4-8 Raw stochastic oscillator and smoothed stochastic oscillator, both with trigger line.

that level. Sell when the oscillator rises above a particular level (for example, 80), and then falls below that level.

2. Buy when the %K rises above the %D. Sell when the opposite happens.

3. Buy or sell when the appropriate divergences occur.

Figure 4-9 illustrates these various methods. The arrows portray method 1. Up arrows indicate a buy and a down arrow a sell. Note that after a sell signal has occurred, a buy signal does not occur until the %K has come below 20, reversed direction, and risen above 20. As can be seen, the crossing of the %K and %D give rise to many more trades and the resulting whipsaws. The divergences, as represented by lines A–A, B–B, C–C, D–D, E–E and F–F, probably lead to the best trades.

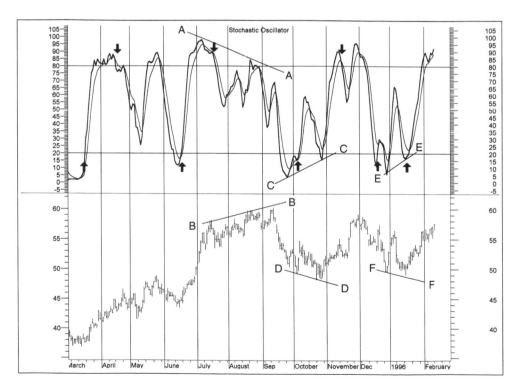

Figure 4-9 Divergent analysis applied to the stochastic oscillator.

DIRECTIONAL MOVEMENT (+DI, –DI, ADX, AND ADXR)

J. Welles Wilder developed a family of indicators that determine which security is most likely to move, which securities are trending, and how fast they are trending. These indicators are labeled +DI, –DI, ADX, and the ADXR.

The +DI measures the directional movement of a security in an upward direction. Similarly, the –DI measures the directional movement of a security in a downward direction. If the +DI goes up, the –DI must go down a similar amount. These indicators can be used to trade. When the +DI goes above the –DI, a buy signal is given, and when the –DI goes above the +DI, a sell signal is given.

Figure 4-10 illustrates this technique. Note that while the +DI and –DI crossover technique confirmed the MACD quite well on the buy

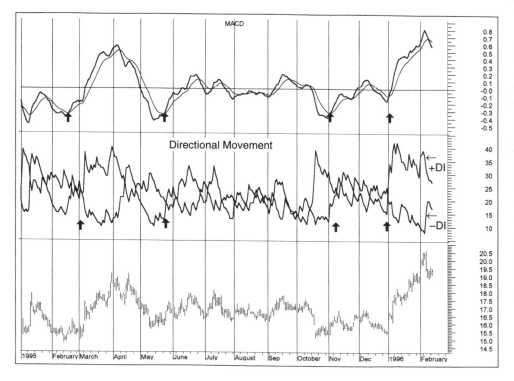

Figure 4-10   Direction movement crossovers compared to the MACD.

side (see arrows), it did a very poor job of confirming sells. This is important because it illustrates the problem of relying on any one indicator, or even any two indicators that do not complement each other.

The ADX measures whether a security is trending. ADXs above 20 usually indicate that a security is in a trend, while ADXs above 50 usually indicate a security that is overdue for a correction. Le Beau and Lucas in their book, *Computer Analysis of the Futures Market*, recommend using the ADX as a filter in mechanical trading systems where the trade should not be entered unless the ADX is above 20. The ADX is always positive. That is, a negatively trending market creates a positive value of the ADX, as does a positively trending market.

Figure 4-11 is a plot of Chubb's stock and the associated ADX. Note how during the trend A–A, the ADX (B–B) continued rising until the stock began consolidating in September. The ADX then began to fall as

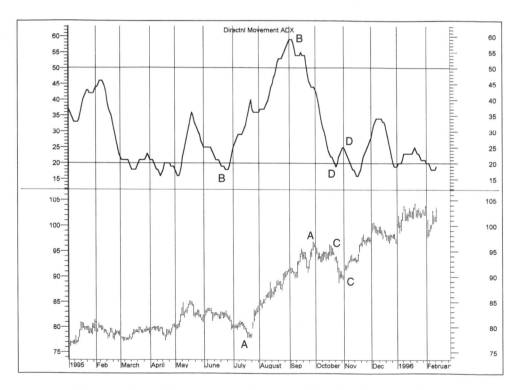

Figure 4-11   ADX indicator and a chart of the Chubb Corporation.

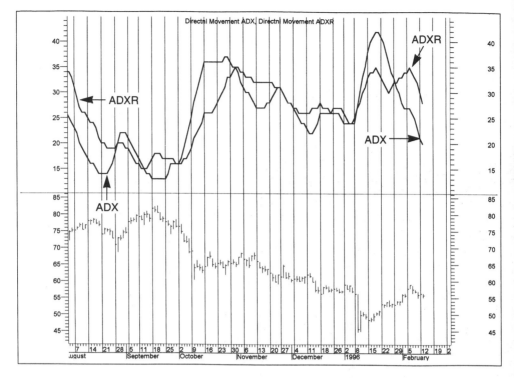

Figure 4-12   A chart of Motorola and the ADXR.

the rate of climb slowed. Also notice that during the fall in prices in period C–C, the ADX began to rise (D–D).

The ADXR is basically a smoothed version of the ADX, as it is an average of today's ADX and that of X number of days ago. Figure 4-12 is a plot of the ADX and ADXR. Note that, as expected, the ADXR is smoother than the ADX.

5

OTHER PATTERNS
AND EVENTS

In this chapter we explore patterns and events that can be used to establish targets and mark the change in a trend.

PATTERNS

Rectangles, Flags, and Triangles

Frequently, prices will rise (or fall) for a while, then move sideways in a consolidating pattern, and finally advance again. Very often when this happens, the second rise has the same magnitude as the first rise. This then gives us a way of targeting the magnitude of the overall advance.

A consolidation pattern can take the form of a *rectangle, flag* (downwards sloping rectangle), or *triangle* (also called *pennants* by some practitioners). Figure 5-1 shows a perfect flag consolidation and subsequent advance. Note that the two advances (line A–A to line B–B and line B–B to line C–C) are identical in both magnitude and time. Both advances are $2\frac{1}{4}$ points and both took 7 trading days to accomplish. Interestingly, the consolidation, which began October 30, also took exactly 7 days, a common event.

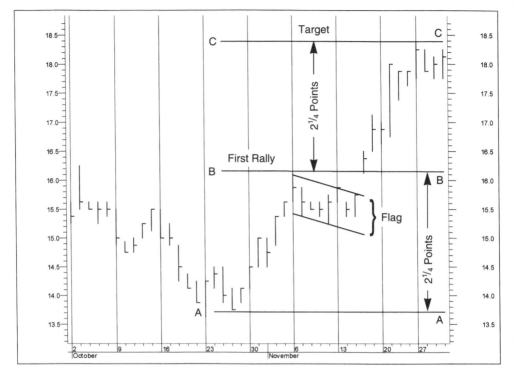

Figure 5-1   Alaska Airlines rallied $2\frac{1}{4}$ points in late October, then went into a flag consolidation pattern. In late November it rallied again another $2\frac{1}{4}$ points. The fact that the two rallies had equal magnitudes is very common and a way of setting ultimate targets.

Figure 5-2 shows a similar pattern (an advance, a consolidation, and another advance), only this time the consolidation pattern is a triangle. Here again the two advances (A–A and B–B, then from C–C to DD) are identical, $2\frac{1}{2}$ points and 11 trading days long. In this case, the consolidation pattern was 12 days long.

Another variation of the triangle or pennant consolidation pattern is one where the triangle has one horizontal side. The side of the triangle that is horizontal almost always shows which way the price will move out of the consolidation pattern. If the flat side is on top, the prices will usually break out to the upside, while if the flat side is on the bottom, the prices will usually break out to the downside. We might interpret the flat side as clear support or resistance, and the angled

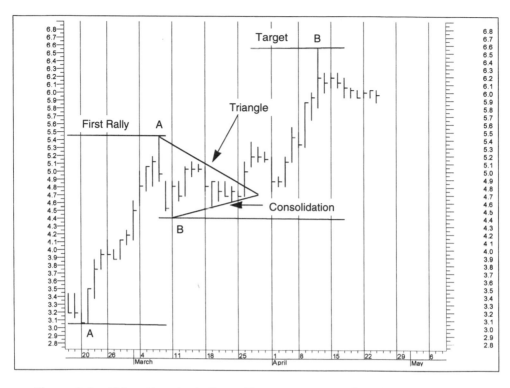

Figure 5-2 This pattern is similar to Figure 5-1, except that the consolidation phase is a triangle rather than a flag.

side as growing pressure to break through that level. Figure 5-3 shows an example of a triangle with a flat top side. Here again, the two advances are almost identical in magnitude with similar, but not identical, periods. In Figures 5-1 and 5-2 daily data were used; in Figure 5-3 weekly data are presented.

Figure 5-4 shows the now familiar pattern, advance–consolidation–advance, only in this case, the second advance is another subpattern of the advance–consolidation–advance pattern. Notice that the advance A–A to B–B is the same size as the advance C–C to D–D. Notice also that the breakout of triangle 1 to F–F, and the breakout of triangle 2 to D–D have similar magnitudes, that is, the moves from the end of triangle 1 to F–F and from triangle 2 to D–D are the same length.

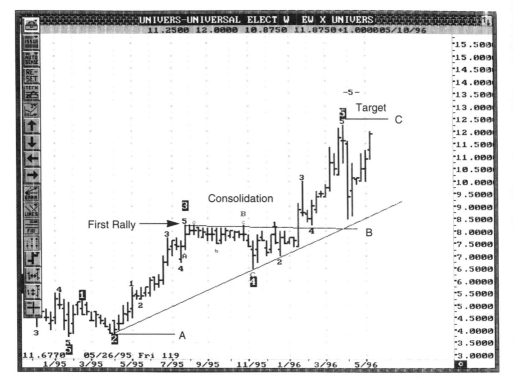

Figure 5-3   This pattern is similar to Figure 5-1, only in this case the consolidation phase is a triangle.

It is interesting to note that the measured amount of retracement (the amount the price goes down during the consolidation period) was exactly 38 percent (a Fibonacci number) in the four patterns presented in Figures 5-1, 5-2, and 5-4.

Flags and triangles appear on charts of all time frames, interday, daily, weekly, monthly, yearly, and so forth. These formations are based on investor behavior and may be considered more important when they apply to charts of bigger proportion.

These patterns appear in both market uptrends and downtrends. When the consolidation process begins following a significant market move, it is possible to target where the market will eventually go. We can then buy or sell as appropriate.

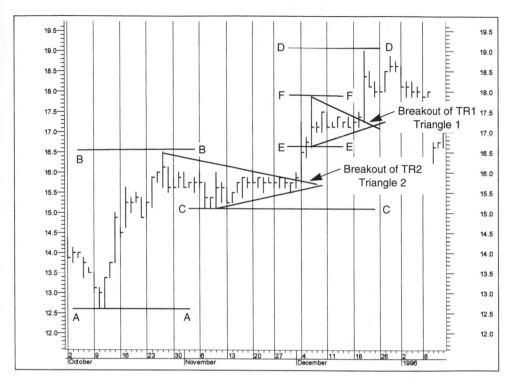

Figure 5-4 Here we have the same pattern as an advance–consolidation–advance, only this pattern is more complex, because the second advance is an advance–consolidation–advance pattern.

Head-and-Shoulders Patterns

A very common pattern marking the end of uptrends or downtrends is the *head-and-shoulders formation*. In Figure 5-5 the H marks the head and the S1, S2, S3, and S4 indicate the shoulders. In this case, double shoulders were formed, a very common variation on the familiar pattern. The head-and-shoulders formation is very popular for establishing a target. Usually, the depth of the head-and-shoulders pattern—the distance between the neckline and the head—indicates the magnitude of the subsequent price movement. In Figure 5-5 the depth (line A–A to line B–B) is the same as the subsequent price movement (line B–B to line C–C). Although the popularity of this pattern may contribute to its success, it is clearly a measurement of volatility.

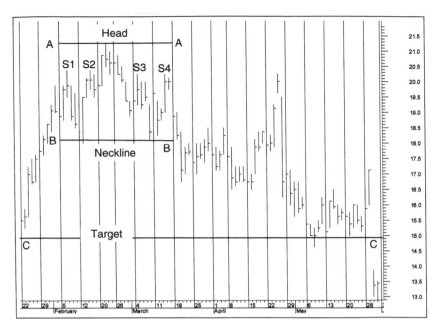

Figure 5-5 An example of a head-and-shoulders top. Note how the decline can be targeted because it is equal to the distance from the head to the neckline.

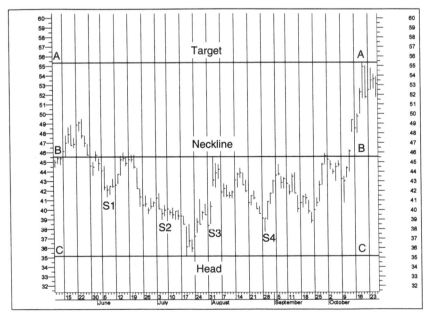

Figure 5-6 An example of a head-and-shoulders bottom. Note how the advance can be targeted.

Figure 5-5 is an example of the head-and-shoulders top, whereas Figure 5-6 is an example of a head-and-shoulders bottom. Here again, the depth (line C–C to line B–B) of the pattern indicates the amount of the next move (line A–A to line B–B).

Double Bottoms and Double Tops

Frequently, prices will fall, then rise, only to fall again, and then rise again, forming a *double bottom*. Prices may as easily do the reverse to produce a double top. Double bottoms, like their cousins head-and-shoulders bottoms, can be used to establish price targets. In Figure 5-7, the double bottom is represented by 1 and 2. The depth of the pattern is shown by lines A–A and B–B. The target price, shown by line C–C is

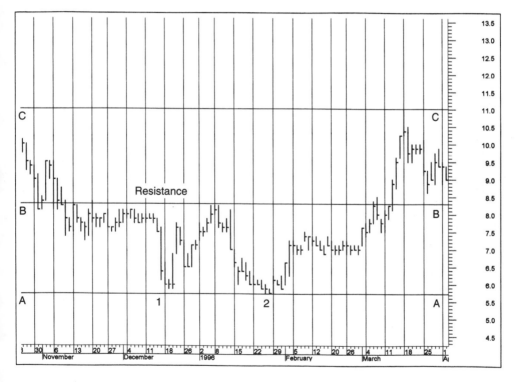

Figure 5-7 Here we have a double bottom. As with a head-and-shoulders pattern, the probable advance can be targeted by measuring the distance from the bottom to the resistance line.

again the same magnitude as the depth of the pattern. Note that prices came up and touched the target level, C–C, and then backed away. The place to draw line B–B is not always as clear for the prolonged bottom as it is for the head-and-shoulders formation. In the case of Figure 5-7, the peak between the bottoms is at about the same level as the previous resistance, but on many charts the patterns are irregular. The best approach is to remember that we are estimating volatility.

Triple Tops and Bottoms

Triple tops (Figure 5-8) and bottoms (Figure 5-9) can be thought of as head-and-shoulders patterns that did not do a good job of forming the head. As with head-and-shoulders patterns, triple tops and bottoms can be used to establish price targets. In Figure 5-8, which illustrates

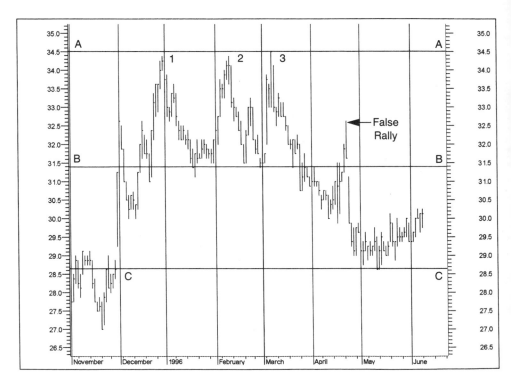

Figure 5-8   Triple top.

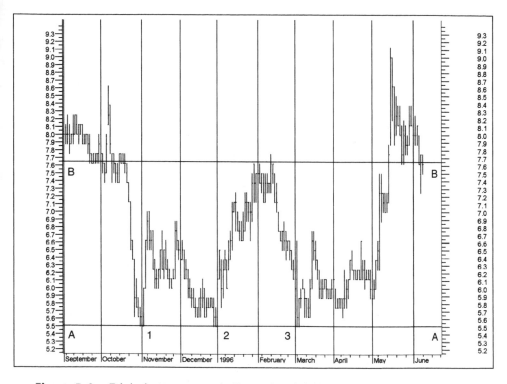

Figure 5-9 Triple bottoms are similar to head-and-shoulders patterns in that the shoulders grow down to meet the head, and like the head-and-shoulders patterns, the probable magnitude of the advance can be targeted.

a triple top, the price broke the neckline at line B–B, came down and touched the target line C–C, and then moved up again. In Figure 5-8, insufficient time has passed since the triple bottom for the price to reach the target, which would be above the chart at approximately 9.7. Note that prices have moved back under level B–B, just as they had in Figure 5-8 during the "false rally." This pattern is not considered as having failed until sufficient time has passed.

EVENTS

There are a number of events that can move the market—including moon phases, day of the week, month of the year, among others—and place it in the option cycle.

Full and New Moons

J. Welles Wilder, who developed the Relative Strength Index, also developed a method of analyzing price data, called *the delta phenomenon*. This method of analyzing leans heavily on the occurrence of full moons. The book describing how to apply the delta phenomenon comes with a separate sheet giving the dates of all the full moons from 1974 to 2000.

Options Expiration

Options expiration, which occurs every third Friday of the month, can often move the market. This is particularly true on the quarterly expiration called *triple witching*, when the stock, futures, and index options all expire on the same Friday. Usually, if options expiration moves the market in a particular direction on late Friday afternoon, this movement is unwound on Monday.

The Monday Phenomenon

Long-term studies have shown that the stock market goes up on Mondays more often than it goes down. Joe Krutsinger, in his book *The Trading Toolkit,* studied this phenomenon in great detail, and found the market went up on Mondays 56 percent of the time. My son, Ted Gately, studied this phenomenon in relation to option expiration and found that during the first two weeks after options expiration, the chance of the market going up on a Monday was 50 percent, and the chance of the market going up on the two Mondays before options expiration was 62 percent. The way to take advantage of this phenomenon is on the two Mondays before options expiration to buy an S&P futures contract on the open and sell it on the close. Krutsinger suggests doing it without a stop, as his simulations using Trade Station show that is more profitable than using a $1,000 stop.

Other Events

Many other events can move the market. Any event that causes uncertainty will drive the market down or up, with greater volatility. When a U.S. president is shot, when the market believes the Federal Reserve will raise interest rates, and when annual earnings are less than expected, the stock market heads down. When the Federal Reserve unexpectedly lowers interest rates and when earnings are better than expected, or the Producer Price Index is unchanged, the stock market rallies.

6

USING FIBONACCI AND OTHER NUMBER SERIES TO ESTABLISH PRICE AND TIME TARGETS

The use of number series to establish price and time targets is an extremely powerful tool, and one that is broadly used by financial analysts. Fibonacci ratios and other number series are found to occur throughout nature, as is shown herein. This chapter illustrates how Fibonacci numbers are developed and how they can be used to determine both price and time targets. It also deals with the importance of the clustering of Fibonacci lines. Other important series are also presented, including the golden proportion series, Gann's series, Carolan's series, and the Rhesus series.

FIBONACCI NUMBERS

The term *Fibonacci numbers* refers to a special numeric sequence where the value of any number in the series is the sum of the two previous numbers; for example, $1 + 1 = 2$, $1 + 2 = 3$, $2 + 3 = 5$, $3 + 5 = 8$,

5 + 8 = 13 and so forth. Each number that follows is explained in terms of Nature's reproduction pattern. The Fibonacci *series* is 1, 1, 2, 3, 5, 8, 13, 21, 34, 55, 89, and so forth.

Figure 6-1 is a drawing of a plant. Note that the number of stems follows the Fibonacci number sequence exactly. Events like this appear many times in Nature.

In addition to the Fibonacci *series*, there are Fibonacci *ratios* derived by dividing adjacent Fibonacci numbers. For example, dividing 55 by 89 equals 0.618, and dividing 34 by 89 equals 0.382. Adding 0.618 and 0.382 together yields 1.000. Dividing 89 by 55 equals 1.618. The sequence of Fibonacci ratios is as follows: 0.38, 0.52, 1.00, 1.62, and so on. Figure 6-2 is an X ray of a Nautilus shell. Figure 6-3 is a drawing of the shell. Note that the ratio of the height of the shell at various points occurs at Fibonacci ratios, again showing the prevalence of Fibonacci numbers and ratios in nature.

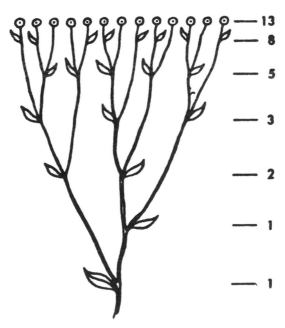

Figure 6-1   Structure of a plant showing that the number of branches are equal to a Fibonacci series.

Figure 6-2 X ray of a Nautilus shell.

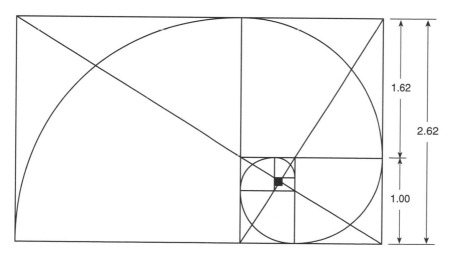

1.62

2.62

1.00

Figure 6-3 Drawing of a Nautilus shell. Note that the ratio of the height of the shell at various points occurs at Fibonacci ratios.

Fibonacci numbers and Fibonacci ratios are very important in technical analysis because advances and declines frequently reverse at points coinciding with Fibonacci numbers or ratios. For example, if an advance is in progress, the chances are quite high that there will be a retracement when the price reaches 1.38, 1.62, or two times the value of the previous advancement. That is to say, that it is highly likely to advance 38, 62, or 100 percent of the previous advance. In the case of declines, very often the decline reverses at a Fibonacci ratio. A 38 or 62 percent decline is very common. In practice Fibonacci

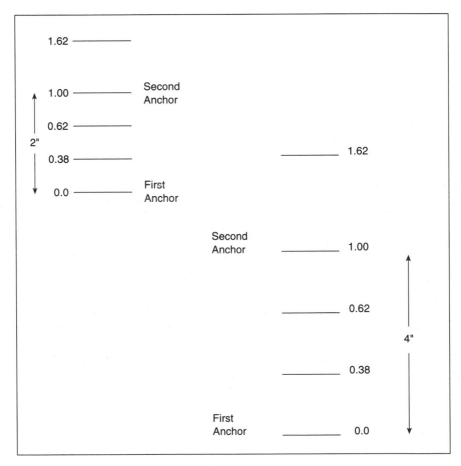

Figure 6-4 Two-inch and four-inch drawing of Fibonacci ratios. Note that regardless of the length of the calipers or anchors, the lines stay proportional.

ratios of 0.382, 0.618, 1.382, 1.618, 2.618, and so on, are the most common.

Fibonacci Numbers as Support and Resistance

The *Nature's Pulse* software program allows data to be enclosed in an *accordion* or *caliper*. These price and time accordions are similar to a computerized proportional divider allowing the analyzing of price support and resistance levels and market timing. The number series used with the accordions can be set by the user.

In practice, click the computer's mouse on the icon for accordions, then select a time or price accordion. Next, select the desired number series and move the cursor via the mouse to the starting point for the accordion, then click the left mouse button. Now move the mouse so that the accordion or caliper encloses the desired data, then lock the data in place by clicking the right mouse button.

Figure 6-4 shows two accordions: the first 2 inches and the second 4 inches. Note that the lines are always proportional to one another.

These accordions can be applied to either price or time data, and are very powerful tools for locating support and resistance zones, as well as projecting where changes in trend might occur.

Fibonacci numbers frequently act as support and resistance zones for the price action. In Figure 6-5, a weekly plot of Infocus Systems, the accordion has been placed around the price movement from A to B, representing a price move from 11 to 33. The numbers 0.38, 0.62, 1.38, and 1.62 represent Fibonacci ratios, or if the decimal point is moved two places to the right, percentages of the distance from A to B. Note that at points marked with an R, resistance was encountered, whereas support occurred at the points marked with an S. Note that these points often correspond to the Fibonacci levels.

Using Fibonacci Numbers to Target Future Prices

Because prices frequently conform to Fibonacci ratios when creating support or resistance zones, it is possible to use Fibonacci numbers to anticipate where an advance might stop. Figure 6-6 shows one set of Fibonacci numbers for one advance of Liberty Corp. Levels 1.38 and 1.62 show likely resistance levels if the advance should become reestablished.

Figure 6-5 Weekly plot of Infocus Systems. An accordion composed of Fibonacci numbers enclosed around the advance from A to B. Note that support and resistance has occurred at various Fibonacci numbers.

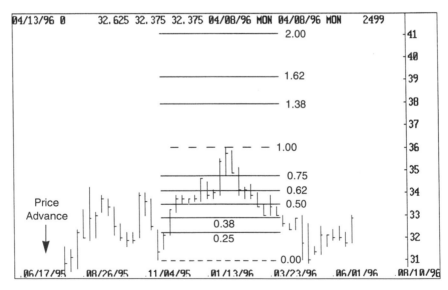

Figure 6-6 Weekly plot of Liberty Corp. The levels 1.38, 1.62, and 2.00 are possible targets if the advance should be reestablished. Note that the fractional Fibonacci numbers have acted as support and resistance.

Clustering

Figures 6-7 and 6-8 show how multiple Fibonacci numbers can be combined to pin down more likely resistance levels. In Figure 6-8 we have placed two sets of Fibonacci ratios around the data, set A–A, B–B around one advance, and set C–C, D–D around a second advance. Note that two lines fall at very nearly the same level, forming a simple cluster at $32.00. Figure 6-9 shows other examples of how the Fibonacci lines cluster. If Liberty's stock should start to advance again, it is highly probable that strong resistance would be encountered at the $37½ to $38.00 levels, cluster I, and even stronger resistance would occur at the $39.00 to $39½ level, cluster II. Also note that a retracement would meet strong support at $32.00 at cluster III; the decline did, however, stop at cluster IV.

Although these illustrations were done on weekly charts, the technique works on charts of any time frame.

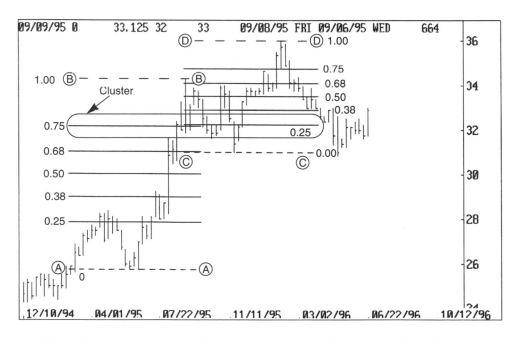

Figure 6-7 Here two accordions have been applied to the data. Note the cluster of Fibonacci lines.

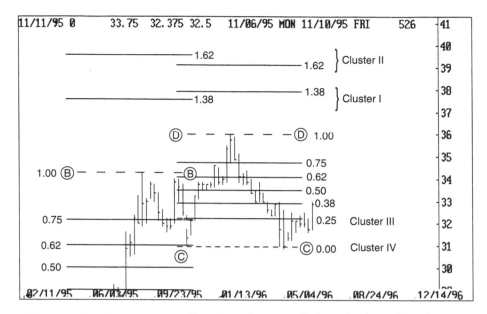

Figure 6-8 Here two accordions have been applied to the data. Four clusters occurred, two establishing support and two establishing possible resistance points.

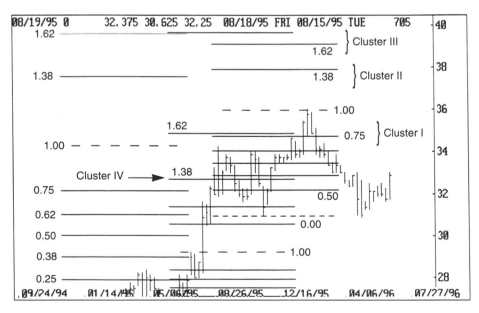

Figure 6-9 Here three accordions have been applied. Note that there are four clusters, three marking possible resistance levels and one a possible support level.

Using Fibonacci Numbers and Ratios to Establish the Timing of Future Changes in Trend

Fibonacci numbers and ratios can also be used to predict when it is likely that a change in trend will occur. We use the ratio to measure and forecast time rather than price. Here we can put the calipers, that is, the 0.00 and 1.00 vertical bars, between two lows: a low and a high, a high and a low, or between two highs. Figure 6-10 is a weekly plot of Lechters stock. Here the basic measurement was between two lows. Note how changes in trend or high volatility bars occurred within a bar of the Fibonacci lines.

In Figure 6-11, a high-to-high measurement has been added to the low-to-low measurement shown in Figure 6-6. Note that this produced clusters of Fibonacci lines at the points labeled A and B. Also note that these clusters appear at points of trend change or of high volatility. This technique can be used to predict future changes in trend, which frequently occur where the Fibonacci lines cluster.

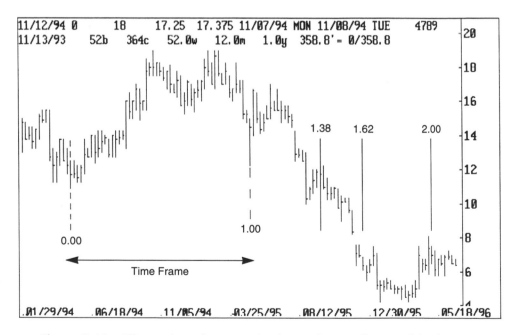

Figure 6-10 Fibonacci numbers can also be used to predict possible changes in volatility. Note the changes in volatility at the Fibonacci points 1.38, 1.62, and 2.00.

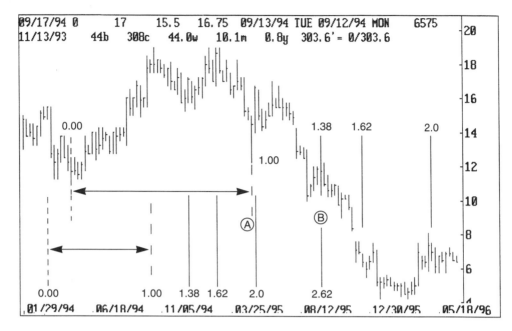

Figure 6-11   Here we have added a second accordion to the data shown in Figure 6-7. Note that there are a number of clusters of the Fibonacci numbers and that these occur at points where the volatility undergoes a change.

Dynamic Fibonacci

As handy as the accordions are, they are of limited use, because eventually the sheer number of lines on the chart becomes overwhelming. To overcome this, the software program called *Nature's Pulse* also contains a program that dynamically applies Fibonacci or other series information to all marked, or chosen, highs and lows and presents the number of clusters without line overkill.

This is accomplished by having the user identify the highs and lows that should be included, and then the program applies the Fibonacci numbers to *all* the possible combinations of chosen highs and lows. Figure 6-12 shows selective highs and lows for IBM and the number of hits each price received, which is how we define the number of Fibonacci lines clustered at that particular price. This information is presented as a frequency distribution plotted sideways at the price.

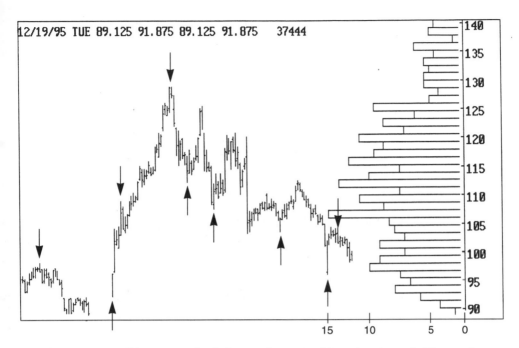

Figure 6-12 Sideways graph of clusters determined by using dynamic Fibonacci-level determination. Note that support and resistance have occurred at the levels with the longest lines.

Figure 6-13 gives the details of this procedure. The first list identifies which dates were selected, the second the series numbers and ratios used, and the third the number of clusters.

This technique of selecting significant levels can be applied to time analysis as well. Using the same turning points identified in Figure 6-13, a time analysis is shown in Figure 6-14. The left part of the graph shown in Figure 6-14 is hidden in order to show the probable future turning points. The turning points are marked with arrows, as was done previously. The bars along the bottom of the chart represent a frequency distribution of the number of hits. The bars lettered A, B, C, and D each had six hits. Since A, B, and C clearly defined previous turning points, it is highly probable that D marks a future change in trend. Bar D is located at September 13, 1996, a Friday. It so happens that when September 13, 1996, came, IBM closed 5 points up from the close of the previous day. This was a change of 4 percent, a very large change in the price of a stock as widely traded as IBM.

C:\MS\DATA\IBM   Int'l Bus. Machi D

The Prices are referenced as "D#"
```
 1    1939   10/10/95H    91.125
 2    1958   11/06/95H    102.38
 3    2006   01/16/96H     87.75
 4    2012   01/24/96H       109
 5    2036   02/28/96H    128.88
 6    2043   03/08/96H    116.88
 7    2050   03/19/96H     125.5
 8    2055   03/26/96H       112
 9    2070   04/17/96H    120.13
10    2085   05/08/96H       106
11    2093   05/20/96H     112.5
12    2106   06/07/96H       102
```

Multipliers as "M#".
```
 1  0.25
 2  0.382
 3  0.618
 4  0.5
 5  0.75
 6  1.382
 7  1
 8  1.618
 9  2
10  3
11  2.618
12  3
13  4
```

Price Cluster Information

Price Hit Ranges	#Hits	Hit Information
87.425 TO 88.752	5	
88.752 TO 90.079	1	
90.079 TO 91.406	4	
91.406 TO 92.732	8	
92.732 TO 94.059	13	
94.059 TO 95.386	10	
95.386 TO 96.713	12	
96.713 TO 98.040	18	
98.039 TO 99.366	16	
99.366 TO 100.69	11	
100.69 TO 102.02	16	
102.02 TO 103.35	11	
103.35 TO 104.67	13	
104.67 TO 106	14	
106 TO 107.33	26	
107.33 TO 108.65	15	
108.65 TO 109.98	20	
109.98 TO 111.31	12	
111.31 TO 112.63	24	
112.63 TO 113.96	18	

Figure 6-13 Lists of data from which Figure 6-12 was derived. The first list gives the dates that were marked upon which the Fibonacci accordions were placed. The second gives the Fibonacci numbers used in the accordions. The last list tells how many hits each price level had.

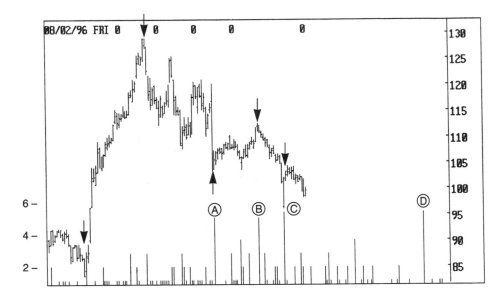

Figure 6-14   Here the dynamic Fibonacci number has been used to mark possible volatility changes. The arrows indicate the dates chosen. Points A, B, C, and D indicate points of probable volatility changes.

OTHER SERIES BASED IN PART ON FIBONACCI

Two series based in part on Fibonacci number series and ratios are frequently used in financial analysis. The first, referred to as the *inside* series, contains the numbers 0.236, 0.382, 0.500, 0.618, and 0.764. It is called inside because all of the numbers are inside the range 0 to 1.000. These numbers are created by dividing a Fibonacci number by the next larger number in the Fibonacci series. In Figure 6-15 the inside series was anchored at the high, point A, and the 0.236 at point B. Note how the 0.382 point fell at the change of trend that occurred at point C. It is probable that changes in trend will occur at points D, E, and F. The second anchor, 1.00, is to the right of the chart.

The second series is called *outside* because all the numbers are outside the 0 to 1 range. These ratios are 1.382, 1.618, 2.618, and 4.136. In Figure 6-16 an accordion using the outside series has been plotted

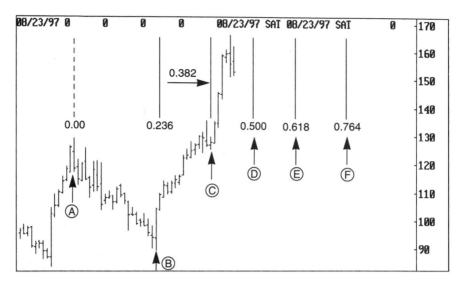

Figure 6-15 An inside Fibonacci line applied to a chart. Here the accordion's first two numbers have been applied to a high and a low, points A and B. Notice the change in trend at point C. Potential changes in trend appear at points D, E, and F. The point 1.00 is off the chart to the right.

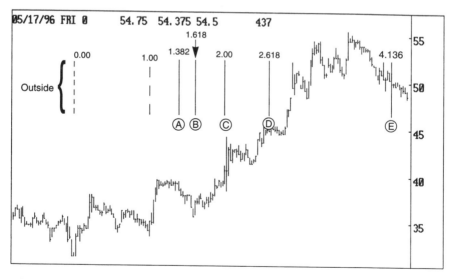

Figure 6-16 An *outside* Fibonacci series applied to a chart. Note the changes in trend at points A, B, and C.

using two lows to anchor the 0.00 and 1.00 points. Note how points A, C, and D line up with highs and point B lines up with a low.

Another Fibonacci-based series is 1, 1, 2, 3, 5, 8, 13, 21, 34, 55, 89, 144, 233, and so on. Each number is the sum of the *two* preceding numbers.

THE GOLDEN SECTION PROPORTION SERIES

Another series that can be used for predicting time and price targets is *the golden section proportion series*, referred to as the *golden series*. This series is derived by multiplying 1.00 by 1.618, then multiplying the product 1.618 by 1.618, then multiplying that product 2.618 by 1.618, and so forth, as follows:

$$1.000 \times 1.618 = 1.618$$
$$1.618 \times 1.618 = 2.618$$
$$2.618 \times 1.618 = 4.236$$
$$4.236 \times 1.618 = 6.854$$
$$6.854 \times 1.618 = 11.09$$
$$11.09 \times 1.618 = 17.94$$
$$17.94 \times 1.618 = 29.03$$

GANN'S SERIES

Gann had several series that he used for predicting when price moves might occur. The first was based on the calendar, or seasons, based on a 360-degree cycle, equal to 365 days, and that contained the following numbers of days: 30, 45, 60, 72, 90, 120, 152, 182, 213, and so on. These numbers are 365 divided by different integers. The major numbers are the 90, 182, 273, and 365 days. Note that Gann's application works best with crops, which are clearly dependent on seasons. In Figure 6-17 we have placed two Gann accordions on the chart, the first using two highs and the second from a high to a low. Note the clustering at point A, and that the 90 point on the upper accordion marks a change in trend, as does the 45 point on the lower accordion.

A second series that Gann used is based on the square of the numbers 1 to 12, which yield the series: 1, 4, 9, 16, 25, 36, 49, 64, 81, 100, 121, and 144. In Figure 6-18 this Gann series has been applied to a

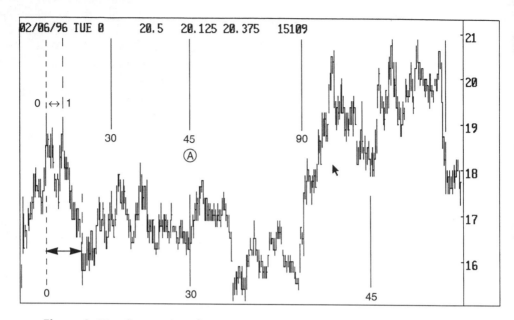

Figure 6-17 Gann series of 30, 45, 60, 90, 120, 152, 182, 213, and so on. Two different time frames were used. Note that there are several clusters.

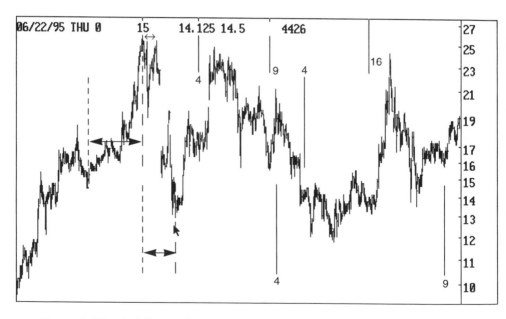

Figure 6-18 A different Gann series, consisting of the square of the numbers 1 to 12, or 1, 4, 9, 16, 25, 36, and so on.

TABLE 6-1 Carolan Numbers

Fibonacci Number	Square Root	Carolan's Number
1	1	29.5
2	1.41	41.8
3	1.73	51.1
5	2.24	66.0
8	2.83	83.5
13	3.61	106.5
21	4.58	135.3

chart of Homestake Mining. Here, as in the first case, this series seems to be almost as good as the Fibonacci series in defining changes in trend.

CAROLAN'S SPIRAL CALENDAR

We can all accept the premise that the gravitational pull of the moon creates physical phenomena, the most significant of which are tides. This can be considered similar to seasonality in its effects.

The Carolan spiral calendar is based on the orbit of the moon around the earth, which takes 29.5 days. To obtain a sequence, 29.5 is multiplied by the square root of the Fibonacci numbers. The calculations are shown in Table 6-1.

Carolan's sequence can be used on weekly charts by dividing the numbers by 7; for monthly charts, divide the sequence by 30.417 (365/12).

RHESUS

Kasanjian Research has developed a Fibonacci-based sequence that they call Rhesus. The sequence is 1.27, 1.62, 2.06, 2.62, 3.33, and 4.24.

7

POSITIONING A STOP-LOSS AND PROFIT OBJECTIVE

This chapter is devoted to methods for establishing levels at which to limit losses, and for establishing points at which to take profits. These price levels can be located using support and resistance levels, trendlines, Fibonacci numbers, or applying values found in other special ratios or series. When these various techniques yield nearly identical price levels, satisfying the concept of clustering discussed in the previous chapter, then they can be very powerful predictors of future prices.

TOO LOOSE VERSUS TOO TIGHT

We do not discuss the use of risk control based on a maximum dollar loss, or a percent of an investment, but focus on levels related to price patterns or expected patterns. If a very close ("tight") stop is set, it is possible that the stop will be hit simply due to random motion of the price, or market "noise." If the stop is set too far from the current price action ("loose"), the loss, when it occurs, may be much too large for prudent money management. It is important to realize close stops lead to a larger number of losing trades. Setting stops is a lesson in choosing the lesser of two evils; we don't want to be out of a trade that is destined to be a big profit, but we don't want to sit quietly on the sidelines while we accumulate a large loss. Using a more analytical approach, as discussed in this chapter, would be welcomed.

SETTING A RISK OBJECTIVE

The most obvious way to set stops is to decide how much money is an acceptable loss. For example, if we have 100 shares of a $50.00 stock, and we decide that we can afford to lose $500.00 on the trade, then the stop-loss point would be set at $45.00, or $5.00 per share. This has the advantage of limiting the loss, but is not a very sophisticated approach to setting stops.

USING SUPPORT LEVELS TO DETERMINE THE STOP-LOSS LEVEL

Support and resistance were explained in Chapter 3. Support is the level at which buyers come in the market, and resistance is the level at which sellers start to sell. Setting stop-loss points slightly below support levels is a popular method of protecting trading capital, because the chances are good that the support will continue to hold and the stop will not be reached. As was explained earlier, resistance levels turn to support levels after they have been breached, and can be used as reference points to set stops.

In Figure 7-1, a weekly chart of American Barrick, there is well-established resistance at the $27.50 level, as shown by the points labeled A, B, and C. However, in January 1996 this level was breached, and it became a support level, as shown by points D and E. In this case, setting stop-loss in the area of $26.50 to $26.75 would be prudent, because if the $27.00 level is seriously broken, then the next support level would be at $23.50 at the point labeled F.

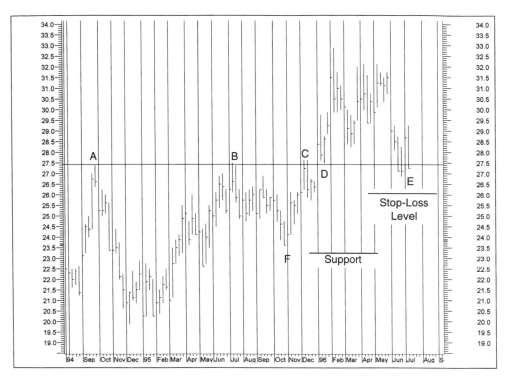

Figure 7-1 At points A, B, and C, $27.375 acted as resistance. In January 1996 this level was breached and this level begin to act as support. Because of this support, a stop-loss could be entered in the neighborhood of $26.50.

USING TRENDLINES TO ESTABLISH
STOP-LOSS POINTS

Another common way to establish stop-loss points is to place them slightly under a trendline. In Figure 7-2, a weekly chart of Alcoa Aluminum, the trendline shown is more than a year in duration, making the breaking of the line a major change of trend. Point C is at $56.00; therefore, a stop placed at $55.00 would be appropriate to protect the profits that have been earned since March of 1995.

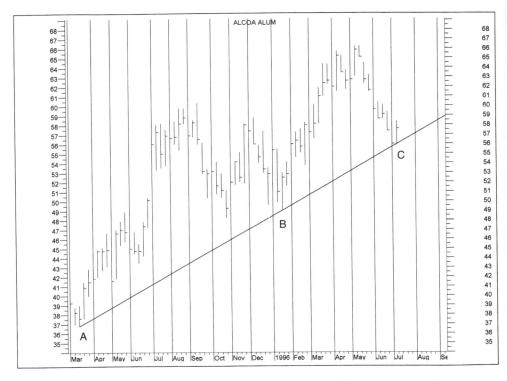

Figure 7-2 Long-term trendlines can be used to establish where stop-loss orders can be entered. Here a stop-loss order at point C could be entered at a level of $55.00.

USING FIBONACCI NUMBERS TO ESTABLISH STOP-LOSS POINTS

Using the Fibonacci accordions, which were discussed in Chapter 6, is an excellent way to find appropriate levels at which to set stop-loss points. In Figure 7-3, Fibonacci accordions have been added to the chart of Alcoa Aluminum. Notice that lines A–A, B–B, C–C, and D–D are within one dollar of each other in the $55.00 to $56.00 range. Also line C–C represents a 38 percent retracement of the 15-month advance. If a wider stop is desired, then a stop at about $53.00, where lines E–E, F–F, and G–G congregate, would be another good level. A third possible area for a stop would be at $52.00 where lines H–H and I–I lie. This

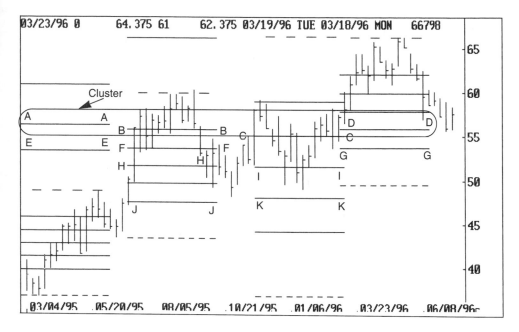

Figure 7-3 The cluster of lines A–A, B–B, C–C, and D–D at $56.00 indicates that strong support exists at that level. A stop at $55.00 would be appropriate. This confirms the level of $55.00 determined in Figure 7-2.

has the added confirmation of a 50 percent retracement of the 15-month advance. Lines J–J and K–K represent a 62 percent retracement of the advance, and would be another likely point to place a very wide and loose stop.

The process of using Fibonacci stops is to first determine where the clustering occurs, and then to determine which level to use. Do not decide to use an odd level with low confirmation, because of the greater risk. Better to skip the trade.

PARABOLIC STOPS

The parabolic time/price system was developed by J. Welles Wilder. This indicator is used to set price stops and is often called the stop-and-reversal (SAR) indicator.

The parabolic calculation results in a series of trailing stops that, if hit, indicate a trend reversal. That is to say, in a rising market, if the stop is hit, the position is reversed from long to short. These stops are recalculated every day and get tighter as time progresses. If the trend fails to continue, the moving stop will reverse the position and a new time period begins. The parabolic is a reversal system that is always in the market.

The formula for SAR is as follows: SAR (tomorrow) = SAR (today) + AF × EP − SAR (today), where AF is the acceleration factor and EP is the extreme high or low point for the prior trade. The previous extreme price and the acceleration factor combine to keep the SAR close to the trend. The AF is a constantly changing weighting factor. Wilder's initial value was 0.02, so each time a new extreme price is reached the ac-

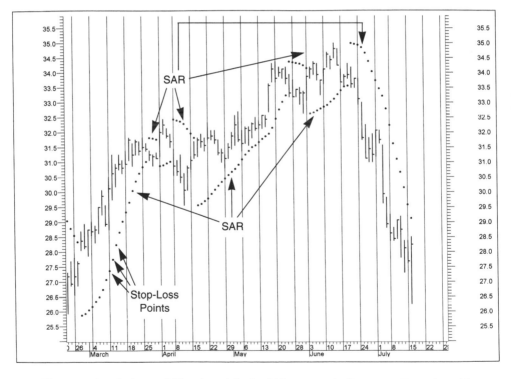

Figure 7-4 A chart of Chrysler with the SAR, or parabolic stops. Note that this method stays with trends and does a good job of getting the investor out of trades when the trend changes.

celeration factor is increased by 0.02. Of course, other values of the acceleration factor can be used, but the 0.02 value suggested by the inventor is the most popular.

If you are long (i.e., the price is above the SAR), the SAR will move up every day, regardless of the direction the price is moving. If you are short (i.e., the price is below the SAR), the SAR moves down each day. The amount of movement is determined by how much and in what direction the price moved.

Figure 7-4 is a daily chart of Chrysler with the SAR plotted on the chart. Note that sometimes the SAR is above the price, and sometimes below. The SAR below is used when long, and the SAR above is used when short. Also, note on the right side of the chart that the amount the SAR is falling accelerates because the price has been falling quite fast. The SAR always eventually catches up to the price, regardless of the speed of price movement. The SAR is a stop system that minimizes seesawing, yet stays with the trade when the security is trending.

USING BANDS AS A METHOD OF SETTING STOPS

Another method of setting stops is to use bands, and set the stop at or slightly below/above the band. As with the trendlines previously discussed, the breaking of a band usually indicates a change in trend. Among possible bands are displaced moving averages, Raff channels, and the Bollinger bands.

Figure 7-5, a chart of Chrysler, shows a 5-day moving average of lows displaced 3 days to the right. Stops should be set below the moving average. Notice that, as with the SAR, this technique stays in the trade while the security is trending.

Figure 7-6 is a 5-day moving average of lows displaced 0.8 percent downwards. Stops would be placed below the moving average. If short, the moving average would be displaced upwards, and the stop placed above the moving average. Note that as with the SAR and the horizontally displaced moving average, this technique stays in the trade when the price is trending.

The heavy line in Figure 7-7 is a Bollinger band using a 5-day moving average with a 1.3 deviation. The light line is the 5-day moving average. Compare the Bollinger band of Figure 7-7 to Figures 7-4 through

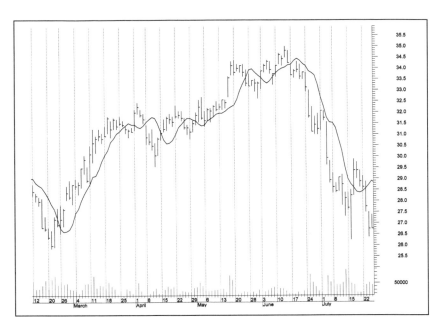

Figure 7-5   A horizontally displaced moving average used to indicate possible stop-loss points.

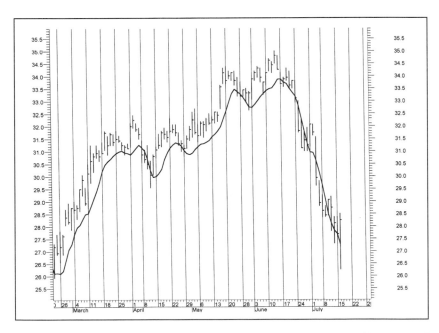

Figure 7-6   A vertically displaced moving average used to indicate possible stop-loss points.

114

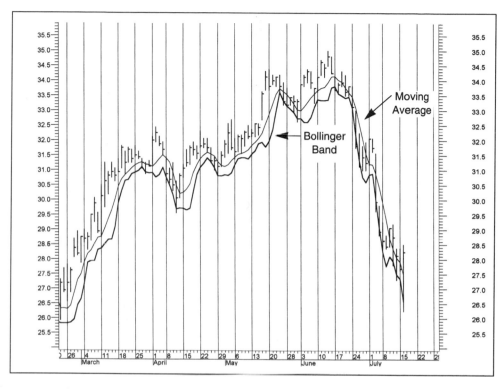

Figure 7-7 Bollinger band used to indicate possible stop-loss points.

7-6. Note that the SAR, displaced moving averages, and the Bollinger band all give stops very close to each other and tend to stay in trends and get out fast when the trend reverses. The moving averages, displacements, and deviation are not written in stone, and other values may be substituted, if tighter or looser stops are desired.

ESTABLISHING TARGETS FOR SELLING USING FIBONACCI LINES

Chapter 6 showed that clusters based on Fibonacci lines were often points where advances or declines stopped and trends reversed. In the case of advancing stocks, these groups can be used to place a sell order in anticipation of a trend reversal.

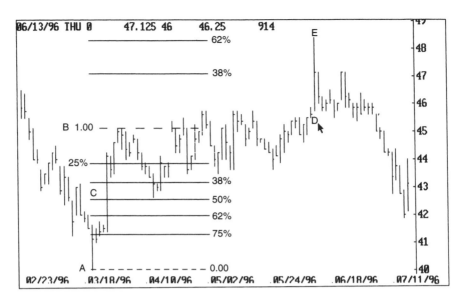

Figure 7-8 Using Fibonacci points to establish possible sell levels. Note that the advance on the right side of the chart went up to the 62 percent Fibonacci point and closed at the Fibonacci level of 38 percent.

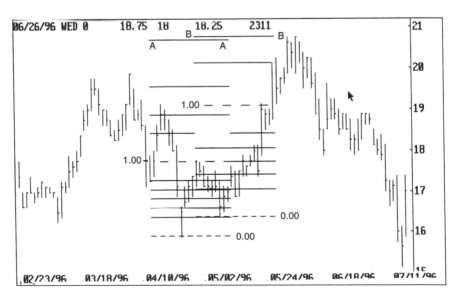

Figure 7-9 Here multiple Fibonacci accordions have been placed on the chart. Note the cluster at $20.75, and that the price reached that level before selling off.

For example, in Figure 7-8 the stock had a good advance from A to B, then went into a consolidation phase, giving up 50 percent of the advance, point C, a Fibonacci point. The stock then consolidated further, until it advanced three points in a day, but could not hold the advance, points D and E. It is interesting that at the peak of the advance it was up an additional 62 percent, a Fibonacci number, and that when it closed that day, it was at 38-percent advance, another Fibonacci number.

In Figure 7-9 Fibonacci accordions have been put around the first two advances. Note that we have a grouping of Fibonacci lines at A–A and B–B. Note also that that is exactly where the trend terminated. By using Fibonacci numbers and observing where numbers cluster, we can identify where the trend will have a higher chance of reversing and put in appropriate stops and sell orders.

8

THE BRADLEY MODEL: GUIDANCE FROM THE STARS?

This chapter is about the Bradley model, a mathematical model of the angular relationships between the planets, and its application to the stock market, specifically the Dow Jones Industrial Average, and is a summation of the manual that Kasanjian Research supplies with their software package for calculating the Bradley model.

To astrologers, the positions of the planets affect the behavior of groups of individuals and can be directly related to market tops and bottoms as well as periods of high volatility. In astronomical terms these planetary relationships are known as *aspects*. Often, changes in the Bradley model occur at the same time as changes in the stock market. Because the Bradley model can be plotted into the future, it becomes another method of timing the market.

The idea that the planets can exert an influence on human behavior does not sit well with most people. The problem is that the planets appear to have some influence on human behavior. In testing the

Bradley model, which we will do subsequently, it is necessary to suspend judgment about how the world works and how laws of Nature govern the outcome of different events around us. It will then be much easier to accept the following conclusion that the Bradley Model of Market Forecasting has worked surprisingly well in the past and continues to work today.

W. D. Gann was considered by many to be a perceptive and successful trader. He had a deep belief that planetary cycles had a strong influence on the agricultural markets. Donald Bradley, the creator of the Bradley model, was more a scientist than a promoter. He cautioned people about thinking he had discovered the answer to calling market turns. It is ironic that his approach is equal to many of today's more popular techniques.

The Bradley model is just a simple, unglamorous plot that appears to be random. As we show later, there is obvious relevance between it and the stock market, and human affairs in general.

That Fibonacci ratios exist in both time and price in the financial markets is believed by many. Fibonacci ratios are also woven into the orbital periods of the planets in our solar system. The Bradley method is calculated on the basis of significant angular relationships between planets. As stated earlier, in astronomical terms, these relationships are known as aspects.

Many people believe that major turns of the market occur at the time of the full or new moon. In fact, a whole methodology has been developed by J. Welles Wilder called *The Delta Phenomenon, or The Hidden Order in All Markets,* which is based on moon cycles. Welles Wilder was also the developer of the Relative Strength Index (RSI) and the parabolic SAR discussed in Chapter 7. To go from full moons to planetary aspects is no great leap, considering that neither case is explainable by what is currently known about the significant forces, or lack thereof, between objects in the cosmos.

What Donald Bradley did was to devise an empirical theory that went beyond the usual mystical language used by astrologers, such as "When the Moon is in the seventh house and Jupiter aligns with Mars, then peace shall reign." Instead, he created a formula that plots the cumulative potency of all planetary aspects in the solar system based upon various weightings. Those weightings are, in turn, based upon the relative distance of the planets approaching toward, and then separating from, significant aspects.

An analogy for this might be a room full of highly strange clocks, each of which keeps time at a different speed. Once in a long while a large number of the clocks will chime at the top of the hour all at once. That's what the Bradley model does. *When a large number of the solar system's orbital clocks chime, the market is predisposed to turning.* That is to say, when the planets are aligned in a certain way, then the market tends to start to trend or change the existing trend.

DOES THE BRADLEY MODEL WORK?

Keeping in mind that the Bradley model is derived from phenomena we normally consider to be independent of the stock market, it would be surprising to find any correlation between the Bradley model and the Dow Jones Industrial Average appearing for an extended period of time. Figure 8-1 shows such a plot for a 16-month period in 1945/1947. A surprisingly good correlation.

Was 1946 a fluke? Figure 8-2 shows another instance during our current century in which the tight correlation between the Dow and the Bradley model have occurred. Analyzing other periods yields similar correlations. While the harmonies between the Dow and the Bradley model are not frequent enough for us to get excited, they do occur often enough for us to conclude that the Bradley model and the U.S. stock market have a relationship that should not be ignored.

BRADLEY FORECAST FOR 1994

In Figure 8-3 we have marked the Bradley plot to show the turning points that show how well those dates corresponded with actual turns in the Dow Jones Industrial Average. Following the dates, in parentheses, are the number of days the actual turn of the Dow differed from the Bradley. For example, 6/27 (–2) means that the actual high or low was on 6/27 and the Bradley model had signaled a change in trend for two trading days earlier.

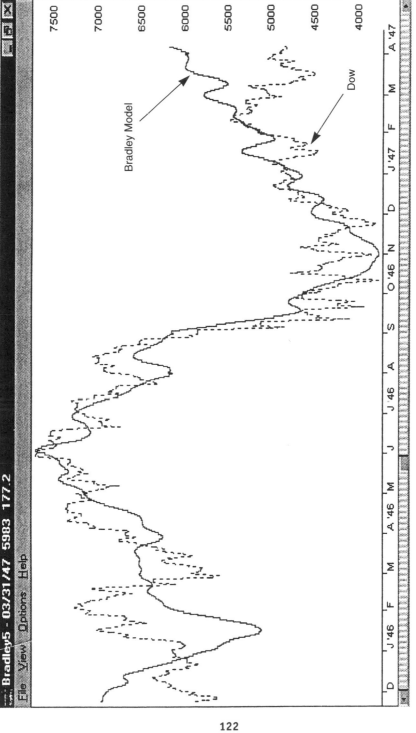

Figure 8-1 Graph of the Bradley model and the Dow Jones Industrial Average for the period December 1945 to April 1947. Note the excellent correlation. The solid line is the Bradley model and the dotted line is the Dow. (Copyright © 1996 by Kasanjian Research. Used with permission from *The Bradley Model for Windows User Manual* by Eddie Kwong.)

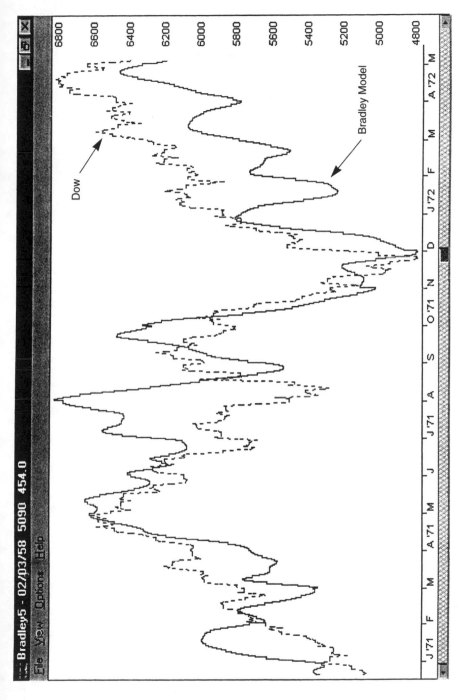

Figure 8-2 Bradley model and the Dow Jones Industrial Average for the period January 1971 to May 1972. The solid line is the Bradley model and the dotted line is the Dow. (Copyright © 1996 by Kasanjian Research. Used with permission from *The Bradley Model for Windows User Manual* by Eddie Kwong.)

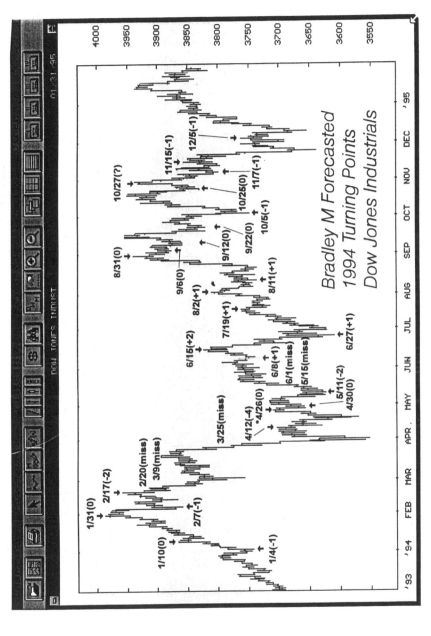

Figure 8-3 Plot of the Dow Jones Industrial Average with comparisons to the turning points predicted by the Bradley model. Following the dates. in parentheses are the number of days the actual turn of the Dow differed from the Bradley. For example: 6/27 (−2) means that the actual high or low was on 6/27 and the Bradley Model has signaled a change in trend two days earlier. (Copyright © 1996 by Kasanjian Research. Used with permission from *The Bradley Model for Windows User Manual* by Eddie Kwong.)

124

THE BRADLEY MODEL AND OTHER
MARKET ANALYSIS TOOLS

The Bradley model is a tool for forecasting turns in the U. S. stock market. It is a system that generates buy and sell signals, but it should be used in combination with other tools that most traders already have in their arsenal. It definitely can be a tool of key importance.

9

USING NEURAL NETWORKS AND GENETIC ALGORITHMS TO ESTABLISH TIME AND PRICE TARGETS

In this chapter we will show the reader how artificial neural networks and genetic algorithms can be used to set price and time targets. The details of using these state-of-the-art methods are beyond the scope of this book, but it is important that the reader be aware that these techniques exist and of the logic behind their use.

NEURAL NETWORKS

All higher-life things have brains composed of cells called *neurons*. These calls are unique in that they do not die, unlike the other cells in an organism. This may account for the fact that we can remember things that took place decades ago. Estimates of the number neurons in the human brain go as high as 100 billion (10^{11}).

The brain is divided vertically into two halves (see Figure 9-1), and the two halves are connected by the corpus callosum, a thick bundle of

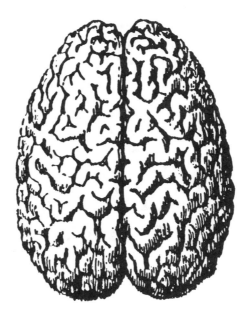

Figure 9-1   Top view of the brain showing division into left and right halves.

nerve fibers. The left side of the brain is devoted to the logical and mathematical functions, while the right side deals with the emotions, pattern recognition, and the intuitive senses. Scientists and mathematicians are said to be left-brain people, while artists and writers are said to be right-brain people.

Technical analysis and fundamental analysis of the financial markets is left-brain oriented, while artificial neural networks (ANNs) act as if they are right-side oriented. An ANN is a computer software program that mimics the human brain's ability to classify patterns or to make predictions or decisions based on past experience, in effect acting like the right side of the brain. The human brain relies on inputs from the five senses, while the ANN uses inputs from data sets.

In the human brain each neuron is connected to many other neurons. Figure 9-2 shows a typical human neuron.

Most ANNs have three or more layers of neurons. The first layer, called the *input layer*, has one neuron for each input to the network. Each neuron in the input layer is connected to every neuron in the second, or *hidden layer*. Each neuron in the hidden layer is connected to the third, or *output layer*. Figure 9-3 shows a simple three-layer net-

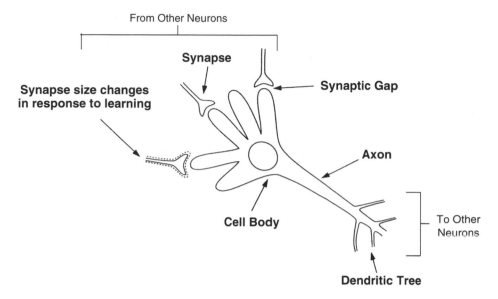

Figure 9-2   Details of a biological neuron.

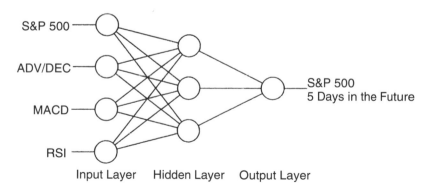

Figure 9-3   Simple three-layer artificial neural network for predicting the S&P 500 five days in advance using today's value of the S&P 500, the Advance/Decline Index, MACD, and RSI as inputs.

TABLE 9-1   Differences Between Human Brain and Neural Network

Factor	Brain	Neural Network
Size	Very large, up to 100 billion neurons	Relatively small, rarely more than a few hundred neurons
Inputs	Five senses	Data sets, reduced to numbers (digitized)
Work ethic	Good, but easily bored and often unfocused	Mechanical, solves only what is asked
Specialization	Yes, but with many interests and skills; can be easily distracted	One task only
Construction	Biological	Mathematical
Interconnections per neuron	Up to 1,000 not uncommon	Limited by state of the art, rarely as many as 100
Brain side	Two, left and right (analytic and intuitive)	Right side only (intuitive)

work using the S&P 500, the Advance/Decline Index, MACD, and Relative Strength Index (RSI) as inputs.

Table 9-1 is a comparison of the human brain and an artificial neural network. As can be seen, the human brain is much more complex when compared to an ANN; however, the ANN can discern patterns that are not obvious to the human brain.

Neural networks are used to recognize patterns and to predict events in the future, such as the price of a stock 5 or 10 periods in the future, when the trend will change, and so forth. Because neural networks are so good at predicting future events, they can be used to predict price and time targets.

GENETIC ALGORITHMS

Genetic algorithms solve optimization problems using the methods of evolution, first put forth by Charles Darwin in 1858, specifically *sur-*

vival of the fittest. The theory is that a population of a certain species will, after many generations, adapt in such a way as to be better suited to its environment. For example, if a species, like a crocodile, lives in a water environment, then those members of the species that have webbing between their toes will be better adapted to the environment than those members whose toes do not have webbing. The members with webbed toes will be able to swim better and thus get more food. If food is in short supply, it is likely that the members without webbed feet will die. If they die, it is likely they did not stay alive long enough to reproduce. However, the crocodiles with webbed feet probably were able to get enough food and live long enough to reproduce. Since it is likely that the genes for webbed feed are in both parents, it is very likely that the children will have webbed feet. Carried on through a number of generations, the species, crocodiles, will have adapted to the water environment by developing webbed feet.

Genetic algorithms solve optimization problems the same way. They create a population of possible solutions to the problem. The solutions will carry "chromosomes" that are the values of the variables of the problem. These solutions are then mated, and most of them die. The children are then mated, and so forth. After hundreds, even thousands of generations, a population eventually emerges where the solutions will solve the problem very well. In fact, the most fit solution will be an optimum or close to an optimum solution to the problem.

Genetic algorithms can, for example, be used to optimize the inputs to neural networks, select a portfolio from a universe of stocks, and establish time and price targets in the security markets.

10

PUTTING IT TOGETHER: UTILIZING A VARIETY OF TECHNIQUES

This chapter is devoted to utilizing multiple techniques to establish price and time targets. In the chapter devoted to Fibonacci series (Chapter 6) we discussed the importance of clusters. If we use a variety of techniques to establish targets, and several of them end up at the same price or time period, then there is a good chance that something will happen at that price or time period.

THE TOOLS

In the previous nine chapters we have discussed a variety of tools that could be used to establish price and time targets, and changes in trend:

Bollinger bands	Cycles
Bradley model	Divergences
Candlesticks	Double bottoms
Channels	Elliott waves

Fibonacci numbers	Moving averages
Fourier analysis	On balance volume (OBV)
Full and new moons	Raff channels
Gann analysis	Rectangles and flags
Head-and-shoulders pattern	Regression analysis
Moving-average convergence/divergence (MACD)	Relative strength index
	Seasonality
	Stochastic

Each analyst has his or her favorite tools and combination of tools, so the following examples are only illustrative of the various techniques involved, not necessarily the only combinations that could be used.

PICKING A SECURITY TO ANALYZE

One way to choose among several securities is to look at one or more of the oscillators. Figure 10-1 shows the MACD of Alaska Airlines. Note the divergence that existed during the July to September period. The price was falling while the oscillator (MACD) was making new highs substantially above the levels reached in early August when the price was much higher than now.

Probably the best method to locate a security to analyze is to find one that has broken a trend line or a resistance level. If looking for a possible short position, the breaking of a support level would be a key event. Figure 10-1 is an example of a security that not only has broken a 3-month trendline but has also broken through a resistance level and is making a 2-month high. The combination of three bullish events— breaking a trendline, pushing through a resistance level, and making a 2-month high—makes this an excellent possibility, if confirmed by other indicators.

Although some stocks move up in a down market, it is better to be in a stock when the market as a whole is moving up. Figure 10-2 is a Bradley model, and it shows a large rise during October, indicating that it is *probable* that the overall market will move up.

Another way to locate possible securities is to use *Investor's Business Daily,* which publishes a list of 60 stocks on the New York Stock

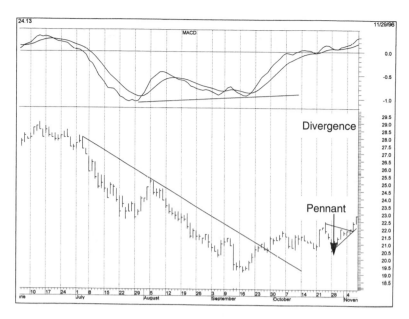

Figure 10-1 Chart of Alaska Airlines with trendline that was broken on September 25th. Chart also includes a pennant in late October. Shown above the chart is a plot of the MACD. Note that the MACD crossover occurred about the time the trendline was broken.

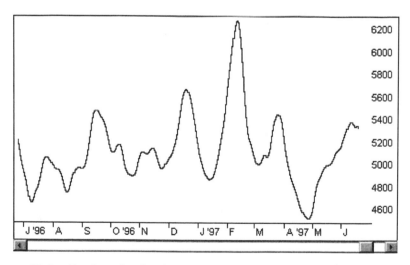

Figure 10-2 Bradley plot for the period covered by Figure 10-1. Note that the period from early November through late December is generally an up-trending period.

135

60 NYSE Stocks With Greatest % Rise In Volume

Compared to stock's last 50 days avg. daily trading volume. Stocks over $15 and ½ pt. change. Stocks up in price listed first. Stocks up with EPS & Relative Strength 80 or more are **boldfaced**.

EPS Rnk	Rel. Str.	Acc. Dis	52-Week High	52-Week Low	Stock Name	Stock Symbol	Closing Price	Price Change	PE Ratio	Float (mil)	Volume (1000s)	% Change In Vol.
81	54	D	22½	18⅝	Stewart Info Svcs	STC	21⅛	+ ¾	9	5.9	236	+2330
37	71	A	18⅛	11½	Hudson Foods Cl A	HFI	17¼	+ ⅞	23	13	877	+1106
75	42	D	34	27⅛	Liberty Financial Co	L	31½	+ ½	10	4.0	89	+787
	56	.	56¾	50⅛	CB United States	GXU	57	+ ⅝	..	0.0	51	+657
49	49	D	55⅝	39	Mckesson Corp o	MCK	49⅜	+ 3⅝	17	43	677	+601
54	75	A	29⅝	21¼	Ahmanson HF&Co o	AHM	30	+ ½	17	106	2,122	+496
43	72	B	15⅞	10¼	GenCorp Inc o	GY	15⅛	+ ½	22	26	340	+486
38	96	A	13¾	6⅞	Comprehensve Care	CMP	15¼	+ 2	..	2.6	151	+433
87	**81**	**B**	**36½**	**21⅞**	**Pep Boys o**	**PBY**	**37⅜**	**+ 1¾**	**25**	**53**	**1,359**	**+410**
89	**89**	**A**	**38¼**	**21½**	**Logicon Inc**	**LGN**	**39⅝**	**+ 1⅞**	**20**	**12**	**138**	**+397**
38	63	B	89	71⅞	Unilever Plc	UL	88	+ 1	18	204	43	+358
91	**96**	**A**	**38½**	**12⅝**	**I T T Educational Svc**	**ESI**	**39**	**+ ¾**	**55**	**3.1**	**51**	**+337**
67	19	D	36⅛	16⅝	Stratus Computer o	SRA	23⅛	+ 3⅜	23	23	536	+337
65	77	B	44⅜	30¼	Reinsurance Grp	RGA	45⅛	+ 1⅜	15	5.9	46	+330
73	58	C	35⅜	24⅞	Coast Savings Fiancl o	CSA	32⅝	+ ¾	15	18	264	+327
88	49	B	20¾	15½	Factset Rsearch Sys	FDS	20½	+ ½	36	10	87	+309
14	63	D	20⅛	15⅜	Ambassador Apart	AAH	19	+ ½	43	7.7	57	+292
80	65	A	34	26½	Legg Mason Inc	LM	33⅜	+ ⅝	12	15	91	+291
77	81	C	61⅜	27½	Guidant Corp o	GDT	52½	+ 3⅛	30	32	1,060	+281
60	52	B	20¾	10⅜	US Air Group o	U	16⅝	+ ⅝	5	63	1,243	+268
65	63	B	41⅛	33⅞	S G L Carbon Aktieng	SGG	40¾	+ 1⅛	23	63	79	+265
26	89	A	21¼	12⅛	Flowers Industries o	FLO	21	+ ½	39	56	572	+264
84	**86**	**A**	**49½**	**14⅞**	**Delta & Pine Land Co**	**DLP**	**38**	**+ ½**	**46**	**16**	**310**	**+253**
81	68	B	23¾	17⅞	Paine Webber Group o	PWJ	23¾	+ 1⅜	7	73	567	+248
93	**88**	**B**	**45½**	**17⅜**	**Total Renal Care**	**TRL**	**43**	**+ 2¼**	**59**	**23**	**130**	**+234**
62	47	B	40¼	28⅝	National Service Ind o	NSI	36⅜	+ ⅞	17	46	353	+230
72	76	B	83½	60¼	Bankers Trust N Y o	BT	81⅞	+ 2	13	79	1,236	+228
88	45	C	34⅞	26⅞	Mutual Risk Mgmt	MM	31	+ 1⅞	17	16	116	+226
88	71	B	64¼	42½	C M A C Investment	CMT	61¾	+ ¾	13	11	98	+225
76	86	A	43⅛	22⅝	Noble Affiliates Inc o	NBL	44⅛	+ 1⅛	57	43	523	+210
76	38	.	19	16⅜	Steinway Musical Ins	LVB	17½	+ 1	32	4.3	311	+209
93	68	D	45½	26⅜	UCAR International	UCR	39⅝	+ ¾	18	18	298	+208
49	73	A	20⅜	11⅜	Scientific-Atlanta o	SFA	17½	+ ⅞	36	77	740	+200
96	63	C	40½	18½	Input Output Inc o	IO	30¾	+ ¾	31	38	501	+194
87	**93**	**A**	**42⅛**	**19½**	**Monsanto Co o**	**MTC**	**41½**	**+ 1⅝**	**29**	**586**	**3,450**	**+194**
92	**84**	**B**	**28**	**17¾**	**Equifax Inc o**	**EFX**	**28¾**	**+ 1⅛**	**25**	**150**	**794**	**+193**
71	62	B	22⅞	17¼	U S X Marathon Grp o	MRO	22¼	+ ⅝	60	285	2,200	+191
74	89	B	31½	19⅝	Comdisco Inc o	CDO	32¾	+ 1⅜	17	36	232	+178
40	65	B	31⅜	24½	Pacific Enterprises o	PET	31	+ ¾	..	83	346	+172
81	67	B	40¼	25¾	Alberto – culver cl a	ACVA	37½	+ ⅞	18	10	64	+158
67	71	B	31	19⅜	Smiths Food&Drug B o	SFD	28	+ ⅝	8	4.8	108	+154
64	75	B	44⅝	34⅝	Corestates Finl Corp o	CFL	45	+ ¾	15	218	961	+149
51	77	B	46	27¼	Melville Corp o	MES	43⅞	+ ½	19	103	1,187	+144
31	24	B	42⅛	26	British Gas Plc	BRG	29⅞	– 1¼	15	421	993	+1558
68	45	B	56⅛	41½	Raytheon Co o	RTN	49	– 4	14	232	4,890	+886
68	58	B	43¾	30⅛	Dole Food Co Inc o	DOL	40⅛	– 2⅞	21	46	1,455	+593
82	36	C	36	26⅜	Trinova Corp o	TNV	30	– 1	9	28	570	+574
34	47	E	22	12⅜	Heritage Media Cl A	HTG	17	– ⅝	22	32	401	+297
26	56	C	56¼	34½	Case Corp o	CSE	47⅛	– ⅞	10	72	1,037	+256
99	19	D	32¾	19¾	Pohang Iron & Steel	PKX	21	– ⅝	6	247	212	+227
66	47	A	44⅛	30⅞	Parker – Hannifn Cp o	PH	38⅛	– 2⅜	12	71	666	+216
95	77	B	34⅛	18⅜	Telekom Indo o	TLK	32	– ½	34	467	226	+205
72	40	C	57¾	36⅞	Hewlett – Packard o	HWP	43⅜	– 1⅞	17	726	9,434	+193
87	65	B	43⅜	30⅞	Wolverine Tube Inc o	WLV	41¾	– 1⅛	17	6.5	109	+170
99	78	B	47	19½	Excel Communictns o	ECI	33¾	– 1⅛	34	29	513	+168
32	15	D	30⅛	19¼	Donna Karan Intl Inc	DK	20⅝	– 1⅝	29	21	530	+164
62	14	C	77⅜	44¾	Motorola Inc o	MOT	48¼	– 1⅜	18	575	6,286	+164
70	79	B	51¼	30½	ENi SPA	E	47⅞	– 1⅛	15	800	64	+163
	19	B	27¾	19⅝	Thai Fund Inc	TTF	20⅜	– ½	..	13	122	+148
13	62	B	44⅛	28½	A K Steel Hldg o	AKS	39⅞	– ¾	5	26	344	+144

Figure 10-3 Example of the listing of possible buy candidates from *Investor's Business Daily*.

Exchange that showed the greatest percent rise in volume. Those that have the greatest relative strength (relative to the market as a whole, not Relative Strength Index (RSI)) are listed in boldface type. Figure 10-3 is an example of the list published daily by *Investor's Business Daily*.

Also in Figure 10-1, note that the consolidation phase, which occurred in October, was in the form of a pennant. Recall that pennants are powerful formations that frequently lead to another rise equal to the first rise.

In Figure 10-4 a Fibonacci caliper has been added. Note that the 2.0 Fibonacci point is clustered with the resistance from August. We now have three separate items that suggest we can target $25.00: the pennant that frequently forms halfway up an advance, the resistance that exists at $25.00, and the Fibonacci level 2. In addition we have a strong advance happening as the price broke a 3-month trendline and a resistance line at $22.00, and divergence in the price versus MACD.

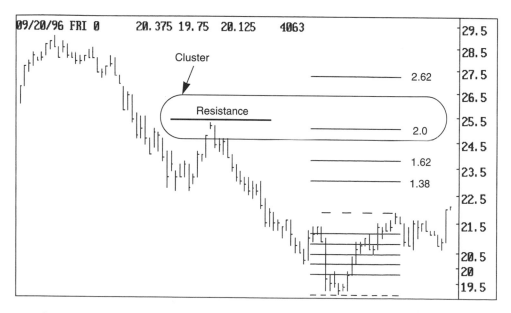

Figure 10-4   Fibonacci caliper added to the plot of Alaska Airlines. Note that the Fibonacci line 2.0 is clustered with the resistance that exists at $25\frac{1}{4}$.

DETERMINING WHEN THE TARGET PRICE
WILL BE REACHED

As important as it is to use targeting methods to project where a security is headed, it is equally important to have an idea of when the target might be reached. The best way to do this is to use Fibonacci and cycle analysis.

Figure 10-5 is a chart of Alaska Airlines stock. Using Fibonacci analysis as described in Chapter 6, the first date with multiple hits is December 24th. December 24th is also the date of the full moon.

Figure 10-6 shows Alaska Airlines stock with cycle lines added. The cycle lines are indicated with arrows. The other lines are date lines. Notice how well the cycle lines indicate the recent breakout. Figure 10-7 shows the cycle lines in the future. The line marked A is on December 17th.

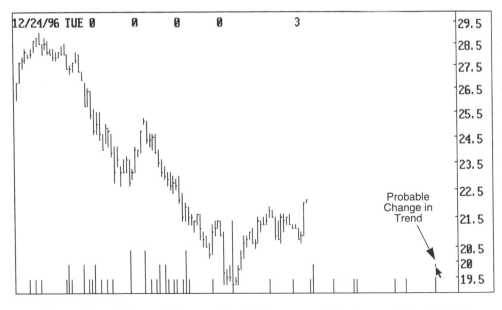

Figure 10-5   Fibonacci time studies indicate a possible change in trend in late December.

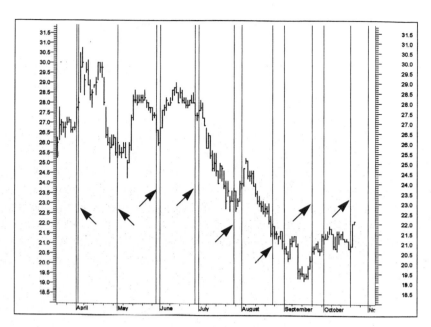

Figure 10-6 Cycle lines have been added to the chart of Alaska Airlines. The arrows indicate the cycle lines. The other lines indicate the change of the month.

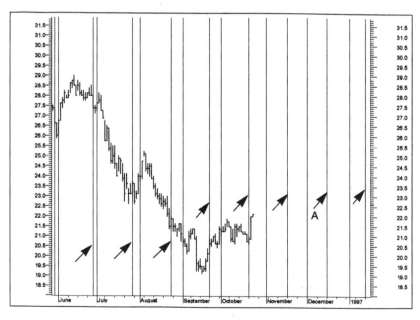

Figure 10-7 Cycle lines extended into the future. Note the cycle line in mid-December that correlates with the Fibonacci line in Figure 10-5.

This is close enough to the December 24th date predicted by the Fibonacci study and the full moon to say that it is likely a change in trend will occur the week before Christmas.

In this chapter we have used a variety of tools to target the probable price and time that Alaska Airlines stock will reach $25.00, that is, the week of December 17 to 24, 1996. The methods selected represent only one of hundreds of possible combinations of the tools available. Each practitioner has his or her own favorite combination of tools.

Targeting the price levels at which changes in trend may occur is very important because it allows preplanning about where to put sell orders and stop-loss orders. Targeting therefore allows the development of alternate plans, which is a much better strategy than *reacting* to unexpected events.

APPENDIX

SOFTWARE USED
IN WRITING THIS BOOK

Metastock for Windows, Version 5.1. EQUIS International, 3950 South 700
East, Suite 100, Salt Lake City, UT 84107, (800) 882-3040. *Metastock for
Windows* is a registered trademark of EQUIS International.

Nature's Pulse, Version 4.0. Kasanjian Research, P.O. Box 4608, Blue Jay, CA
92317-4608, (909) 337-0816. *Nature's Pulse* is a registered trademark of
Kasanjian Research.

Bradley Model. Kasanjian Research, P.O. 4608, Blue Jay, CA 92317-4608, (909)
337-0816. *Bradley Model* is a registered trademark of Kasanjian Research.

G.E.T., Version 5.0. Trading Techniques, Inc., 677 W. Turkeyfoot Lake Road,
Akron, OH 44319, (330) 645-0077. *G.E.T.* is a registered trademark of
Trading Techniques.

NeuroShell 2. Ward Systems Group, Executive Park West, 5 Hillcrest Drive,
Frederick, MD 21702, (301) 662-7950. *NeuroShell 2* is a registered trademark of Ward Systems Group.

GeneHunter, Ward Systems Group, Executive Park West, 5 Hillcrest Drive,
Frederick, MD 21702, (301) 662-7950. *GeneHunter* is a registered trademark of Ward Systems Group.

BIBLIOGRAPHY

Aan, Peter W. "How RSI Behaves," *Futures,* January 1985.

Abraham, Bovas, and Johannes Ledolter. *Statistical Methods for Forecasting,* Wiley, New York, 1983.

Abramowitz, Milton, and Irene A. Stegun, eds. *Handbook of Mathematical Functions,* Dover, New York, 1972.

Adler, P. A., and P. Adler. *The Social Dynamics of Financial Markets,* JAI Press, Greenwich, CT, 1984.

Ainsworth, Ralph M. *Profitable Grain Trading,* Traders Press, Greensville, SC, 1980 (originally published 1933).

Anderson, James A., Andras Pellionisz, and Edward Rosenfeld, eds. *Neuro-computing 2,* MIT Press, Cambridge, MA, 1990.

Anderson, Philip W., Kenneth Arrow, and David Pines, eds., *The Economy as an Evolving Complex System,* Sante Fe Institute Proceedings, vol. V, Addison-Wesley, Redwood City, CA, 1988.

Andrews, W. S. *Magic Squares and Cubes,* Dover, New York, 1960.

Angas, L. L. B. *Investment for Appreciation,* Somerset, New York, 1936.

Angell, George. "Thinking Contrarily," *Commodities Magazine,* November 1976 (an interview with R. Earl Hadady).

Angell, George. *Winning in the Commodities Markets,* Doubleday, New York, 1979.

Angell, George. *Winning in the Futures Markets,* Probus Publishing, Chicago, 1990.

Angly, Edward. *Oh Yeah?* Fraser, Burlington, VT, 1988 (originally published in 1931 by the Viking Press).

Appel, Gerald. *Winning Market Systems: 83 Ways to Beat the Market,* Signalert, Great Neck, NY, 1974.

Appel, Gerald. *Day-Trading with Gerald Appel* (video), Financial Trading Seminars, Inc., New York, 1989.

Appel, Gerald, and Martin E. Zweig. *New Directions in Technical Analysis,* Signalert, Great Neck, NY, 1976.

Ariel, Robert A. "High Stock Returns before Holidays: Existence and Evidence on Possible Causes," *Journal of Finance,* vol. XLV, no. 5, pp. 1611–1626, December 1990.

Arms, Richard W., Jr. "Equivolume—A New Method of Charting," *Commodities Magazine,* April 1973.

Arms, Richard W., Jr. *The Arms Index,* Business One Irwin, Homewood, IL, 1988.

Arnold, Curtis M. *The Personal Computer Can Make You Rich in Stocks and Commodities,* Weiss Research, West Palm Beach, FL, 1980 (hardcover published in 1984).

Arnold, Curtis M. "Your Computer Can Take You Beyond Charting," *Futures,* May 1984.

Arnold, Curtis M. "Tracking 'Big Money' May Tip Off Trend Changes," *Futures,* February 1985.

Aronson, David R. "An Introduction to Computer-Based Pattern Recognition," *Financial and Investment Software Review,* January/February 1984.

Aronson, David R. "Artificial Intelligence/Pattern Recognition Applied to Forecasting Financial Market Trends," *Market Technicians Association Journal,* May 1985, pp. 91–131.

Babcock, Bruce, Jr. *The Dow Jones-Irwin Guide to Commodity Trading Systems,* Dow Jones-Irwin, Homewood, IL, 1989.

Bachelier, L. "Theory of Speculation," in P. Cootner, ed., *The Random Character of Stock Market Prices*, MIT Press, Cambridge, MA, 1964.

Bailey, T. J. *The Elements of Stochastic Processes with Applications to the Natural Sciences,* Wiley, New York, 1964.

Balsara, Nauzer J. *Money Management Strategies for Future Traders,* Wiley, New York, 1992.

Band, R. E. *Contrary Investing,* Viking Penguin, New York, 1986.

Barach, Roland. *MINDTRAPS: Mastering the Inner World of Investing,* Dow Jones-Irwin, Homewood, IL, 1988.

Barnett, Eugene H. *Programming Time-Shared Computers in BASIC,* Wiley-Interscience, New York, 1972.

Baruch, Bernard M. *Baruch: My Own Story,* Holt, Rinehart, and Winston, New York, 1957.

Battley, Nick. *An Introduction to Commodity Futures and Options,* McGraw-Hill, London, 1989.

Belveal, L. Dee. *Charting Commodity Market Price Behavior,* Dow Jones-Irwin, Homewood, IL, 1989.

Bernstein Jacob. "Cyclic and Seasonal Price Tendencies in Meat and Livestock Markets," in Todd Lofton, ed., *Trading Tactics: A Livestock Futures Anthology,* Chicago Mercantile Exchange, 1986.

Beyer, William H., ed., *Standard Mathematical Tables,* 24th ed., CRC Press, Cleveland, OH, 1976.

Bloomfield, Peter. *Fourier Analysis of Time Series,* Wiley, New York, 1976.

Bolton, A. Hamilton. *The Elliott Wave Principle, A Critical Appraisal.* Bolton, Tremblay, Montreal, Canada, 1960.

Bookstaber, Richard. *The Complete Investment Book,* Scott, Foresman, Glenview, IL, 1985.

Bourlard, H., and Y. Kamp. "Auto-association by Multi-layer Perceptrons and Singular Value Decomposition," *Biological Cybernetics,* vol. 59, pp. 291–294, 1988.

Box, G. E. P., and G. M. Jenkins. *Time Series Analysis: Forecasting and Control,* 2nd ed., Holden-Day, San Francisco, 1976.

Brock, William A. "Causality, Chaos, Explanation and Prediction in Economics and Finance," chap. 10 in John L. Casti and Anders Karlqvist, eds., *Beyond Belief: Randomness, Prediction and Explanation in Science,* CRC Press, Boca Raton, FL, 1991.

Brock, William A., David A. Hsieh, and Blake LeBaron. *A Test for Nonlinear Dynamics,* MIT Press, Cambridge, MA, 1990.

Brock, William, Josef Lakonishok, and Blake LeBaron. "Simple Technical Trading Rules and the Stochastic Properties of Stock Returns," Social Systems Research Institute Workshop Series no. 9022, October 1990, University of Wisconsin-Madison.

Bullish Review Newsletter, Rosemount, MN.

Burke, Gibbons. "The Computerized Trader," *Futures,* vol. XXI, p. 74, May 1992; p. 68, July 1992.

Burke, Gibbons. "Perils, Pitfalls and Stumbling Blocks," *Futures,* vol. XXII, no. 3, pp. 30–34, March 1993.

Burrascano, P. "Learning Vector Quantization for the Probabilistic Neural Networks," *IEEE Transactions on Neural Networks,* vol. 2, pp. 458–461, July 1991.

Callen, Earl, and Don Shapero. "A Theory of Social Imitation," *Physics Today,* pp. 23–28, July 1974.

Casdagli, Martin. "Nonlinear Prediction of Chaotic Time Series," *Physica D,* vol. 35, pp. 335–356, 1989.

Casdagli, Martin, and Stephen Eubank, eds. *Nonlinear Modeling and Forecasting,* Sante Fe Institute Proceedings, vol. XII, Addison-Wesley, Redwood City, CA, 1992.

Casti, John L. *Searching for Certainty,* Morrow, New York, 1991.

Caudill, M., and C. Butler, *Naturally Intelligent Systems,* MIT Press, Cambridge, MA, 1990.

Chatfield, C. *The Analysis of a Time Series: Theory and Practice,* Chapman & Hall, London, 1973.

Chen, Ping. "Empirical and Theoretical Evidence of Economic Chaos," *System Dynamics Review 4,* pp. 81–108, 1988.

Church, A. H. *On the Relation of Phyllotaxis to Mechanical Laws,* Williams & Newgate, London, 1904.

Cleeton, Claude. *The Art of Independent Investing,* Prentice Hall, Englewood Cliffs, NJ, 1976.

Club 3000 Newsletter, Augusta, MI.

Cohen, A. W. *How to Use the Three-Point Reversal Method of Point and Figure Stock Market Trading,* Chartcraft, Larchmont, NY, 1972.

Commodity Trading Manual. Chicago Board of Trade.

Commodity Traders Club. *Comparative Performances,* Messena, NY, 1969 (reprint).

Commodity Yearbook 1975. Commodity Research Bureau, NY, 1975.

CompuTrac Software Manual, CompuTrac, New Orleans, LA, 1991.

ContiCommodity. *Seasonality in Agricultural Futures Market,* ContiCommodity Services, Chicago, 1983.

Control Data Corporation. *Control Data 6000 Series Computer Systems Statistical Subroutines Reference Manual,* St. Paul, MN, 1966.

Cootner, P., ed. *The Random Character of Stock Market Prices,* MIT Press, Cambridge, MA, 1964.

Cootner, P. *Speculation and Hedging,* Food Research Institute Studies, vol. VII, 1967 Supplement, Stanford University Press, Stanford, CA, 1967.

Crane, Burton. *The Sophisticated Investor,* Simon & Schuster, New York, 1959 (7th printing).

Crim, Elias. "Are You Watching the Right Signals?" *Futures,* June 1985.

Cycles, Foundation for the Study of Cycles, Pittsburgh, January 1976.

Davis, L. J. "Buffett Takes Stock," *The New York Times,* April 1, 1990.

Davis, Robert Earl. *Profit and Profitability,* R. E. Davis, West Lafayette, IN, 1969.

Davis, R. E., and C. C. Thiel, Jr. *A Computer Analysis of the Moving Average Applied to Commodity Futures Trading,* Ouiatenon Management Co., West Lafayette, IN, 1970 (a research report).

DeVilliers, Victor. *The Point and Figure Method of Anticipating Stock Price Movements,* Trader Press, NY, 1966 (1933 reprint).

Dewey, Edward R., and Og Mandino. *Cycles,* Hawthorne Books, NY, 1971.

Diamond, Barbara, and Mark Kollar. *24-Hour Trading,* Wiley, New York, 1989.

Dimson, E., ed. *Stock Market Anomalies,* Cambridge University Press, Cambridge, England, 1988.

Donchian, Richard D. "Donchian 5- and 20-Day Moving Averages," *Commodities Magazine,* December 1974.

Douglas, Mark. *The Disciplined Trader,* NYIF, New York, 1990.

Downie, N. M., and R. W. Heath. *Basic Statistical Method,* 3rd ed., Harper & Row, NY, 1970.

Dreman, David M. *Psychology and the Stock Market: Investment Strategy Beyond Random Walk,* AMACOM, New York, 1977.

Dreman, David M. *The New Contrarian Investment Straightedge,* Random House, New York, 1982.

Drew, G. A. *New Methods for Profit in the Stock Market,* 2nd ed., Metcalf Press, Boston, 1941.

Duda, R., and P. Hart. *Pattern Classification and Scene Analysis,* 2nd ed., Wiley, New York, 1993.

Dunn, Dennis. *Consistent Profits in June Live Beef Cattle,* Dunn & Hargitt, West Lafayette, IN, 1972.

Dunnigan, William. *One Way Formula,* Dunnigan, Palo Alto, CA, 1955.

Dunnigan, William. *Select Studies in Speculation,* Dunnigan, San Francisco, 1954 (includes "Gain in Grains," and "The Thrust Method in Stocks").

Dunnigan, William. *117 Barometers for Forecasting Stock Price,* Dunnigan, San Francisco, 1954.

Dwyer, G. P., and R. W. Hafer, eds. *The Stock Market: Bubbles, Volatility and Chaos,* Kluwer Academic, Lancaster, PA, 1989.

Earp, Richard B. "Correlating Taylor and Polous," *Commodities Magazine,* September 1973.

Eberhart, Russell C., and Roy W. Dobbins, eds. *Neural Network PC Tools,* Academic Press, London, 1990.

Edwards, Robert D., and John Magee. *Technical Analysis of Stock Trends,* John Magee, Springfield, MA, 1948.

Efron, B. *The Jackknife, the Bootstrap and Other Resampling Plans,* SIAM, Philadelphia, 1982.

Ehlers, John F. "Optimizing RSI with Cycles," *Technical Analysis of Stocks & Commodities,* February 1986.

Ehlers, John F. "Trading Channels," *Technical Analysis of Stocks & Commodities,* April 1986.

Ehlers, John F. *MESA and Trading Market Cycles,* Wiley, New York, 1992.

Elder, Alexander. "Triple Screen Trading System," *Futures Magazine,* April 1986.

Elder, Alexander. *Directional System* (video), Financial Trading Seminars, Inc., New York, 1988.

Elder, Alexander. *MACD & MACD-Histogram* (video), Financial Trading Seminars, Inc., New York, 1988.

Elder, Alexander. *Relative Strength Index* (video), Financial Trading Seminars, New York, 1988.

Elder, Alexander. *Stochastic* (video), Financial Trading Seminar, Inc., New York, 1988.

Elder, Alexander. *Williams %R* (video), Financial Trading Seminars, Inc., New York, 1988.

Elder, Alexander. *Triple Screen Trading System* (video), Financial Trading Seminars, Inc., New York, 1989.

Elder, Alexander. *Elder-Ray* (video), Financial Trading Seminars, Inc., New York, 1990.

Elder, Alexander. "Market Gurus," *Futures and Opinions World,* London, September 1990.

Elder, Alexander. *Technical Analysis in Just 52 Minutes* (video), Financial Trading Seminars, Inc., New York, 1992.

Elliott, R. N. *The Wave Principle,* Elliott, New York, 1938.

Elliott, R. N. *Nature's Law: The Secret of the Universe,* Elliott, New York, 1946.

Elman, J. L. "Finding Structure in Time," *Cognitive Science,* vol. 14, pp. 179–211, 1980.

Elton, E., and M. Gruber. *Modern Portfolio Theory and Investment Analysis,* 4th ed., Wiley, New York, 1991.

Emmett, Tucker J. "Fibonacci Cycles," *Technical Analysis of Stocks and Commodities,* May 1983; March/April 1984.

Engel, Louis. *How to Buy Stocks,* Bantam Books, New York, 1977 (1953 reprint).

Epstein, Richard A. *The Theory of Gambling and Statistical Logic,* revised ed., Academic Press, New York, 1977.

Ericsson, Christina. *Forecasting Success,* Kaufman, Westport, CT, 1987.

Evans, Eric. "Why You Can't Rely on 'Key Reversal Days'," *Futures,* March 1985.

Farmer, J. Doyne, and John J. Sidorowich. "Predicting Chaotic Time Series," *Physical Review Letters,* vol. 59, pp. 845–848, 24 August 1987.

Feller, William. *An Introduction to Probability Theory and Its Applications,* 3rd ed., vol. 1, Wiley, New York, 1986.

Fischer, Robert. *The Golden Section Compass Seminar,* Fibonacci Trading, P.O. Box HM 1653, Hamilton 5, Bermuda.

Floss, Carl William. *Market Rhythm,* Investors Publishing Co., New York, 1955.

Fraser, James L. *10 Ways to Become Rich,* Fraser, Wells, England, 1967.

Fraser, James L. *10 Rules for Investing,* Fraser, Burlington, VT, 1978 (2nd printing).

Freedman, Roy S. "AI on Wall Street," *IEEE Expert,* pp. 3–9, April 1991.

Freud, Sigmund. *Group Psychology and the Analysis of the Ego,* Hogarth Press, London 1974 (1921 reprint).

Friedman, Milton. *Essays in Positive Economics,* The University of Chicago Press, Chicago, 1953.

Frost, A. J., and Robert R. Prechter, Jr. *Elliott Wave Principle,* New Classics Library, Chappaqua, New York, 1978.

Fuller, Wayne A. *Introduction to Statistical Time Series,* Wiley, New York, 1976.

Fults, John Lee. *Magic Squares,* Open Court, La Salle, IL, 1974.

Gabr, M. M., and T. Subba Rao. "The Estimation and Prediction of Subset Bilinear Time Series Models with Applications," *Time Series Analysis,* vol. 2, pp. 155–171, 1981.

Gann, William D. *The Basis of My Forecasting Method for Grain,* Lambert-Gann, Pomeroy, WA, 1976 (originally 1935).

Gann, William D. *Forecasting Grains by Time Cycles,* Lambert-Gann, Pomeroy, WA, 1976 (originally 1946).

Gann, William D. *Forecasting Rules for Cotton,* Lambert-Gann, Pomeroy, WA, 1976.

Gann, William D. *Forecasting Rules for Grain—Geometric Angles,* Lambert-Gann, Pomeroy, WA, 1976.

Gann, William D. *How to Make Profits in Commodities,* Lambert-Gann, Pomeroy, WA, 1976 (originally 1942).

Gann, William D. *Master Calculator for Weekly Time Periods to Determine the Trend of Stocks and Commodities,* Lambert-Gann, Pomeroy, WA, 1976.

Gann, William D. *Master Charts,* Lambert-Gann, Pomeroy, WA, 1976.

Gann, William D. *Mechanical Method and Trend Indicator for Trading in Wheat, Corn, Rye or Oats,* Lambert-Gann, Pomeroy, WA, 1976 (originally 1934).

Gann, William D. *Rules for Trading in Soybeans, Corn, Wheat, Oats and Rye,* Lambert-Gann, Pomeroy, WA, 1976.

Gann, William D. *Speculation: A Profitable Profession (A Course of Instruction in Grains),* Lambert-Gann, Pomeroy, WA, 1976 (originally 1955).

Gann, William D. *45 Years in Wall Street,* Lambert-Gann, Pomeroy, WA, 1976 (originally 1949).

Gannsoft Publishing, "Ganntrader I," *Technical Analysis of Stocks & Commodities,* January/February 1984.

Garland, Trudi Hammel. *Fascinating Fibonaccis,* Dale Seymour Publications, Palo Alto, CA, 1987.

Gately, Edward. *Neural Networks for Financial Forecasting,* Wiley, New York, 1996.

Gehm, Fred. *Commodity Market Money Management,* Wiley, New York, 1983.

Gehm, Fred. "Does Pyramiding Make Sense?" *Technical Analysis of Stocks and Commodities.* February 1986.

Gibson, Thomas. *The Facts about Speculation.* Fraser, Burlington, VT, 1965.

Gies, Joseph, and Francis Gies. *Leonard of Pisa and the New Mathematics of the Middle Ages,* Thomas M. Crowell, New York, 1969.

Gilchrist, Warren. *Statistical Forecasting,* Wiley, London, 1976.

Ginter G., and J. Richie. "Data Errors and Price Distortions," in Perry J. Kaufman, ed., *Technical Analysis in Commodities,* Wiley, New York, 1980.

Gotthelf, Edward B. *The Commodex System,* Commodity Futures Forecast, New York, 1970.

Gotthelf, Phillip, and Carl Gropper. "Systems Do Work . . . But You Need a Plan," *Commodities Magazine,* April 1977.

Gould, Bruce G. *Dow Jones-Irwin Guide to Commodities Trading,* Dow Jones-Irwin, Homewood, IL 1973.

Granville, Joseph. *New Strategy of Daily Stock Market Timing for Maximum Profit,* Prentice-Hall, Englewood Cliffs, NJ, 1976.

Granville, Joseph. *The Book of Granville: Reflections of a Stock Market Prophet,* St. Martins Press, New York, 1984.

Greenson, Ralph R. "On Gambling," in *Explorations in Psychoanalysis,* International Universities Press, New York, 1978 (1947 reprint).

Greising, David, and Laurie Morse. *Brokers, Bagmen, & Moles,* Wiley, New York, 1991.

Grossberg, S. *Studies of the Mind and Brain,* Holland, Reidel Press, Dordrecht, The Netherlands, 1982.

Grushcow, J., and C. Smith. *Profits Through Seasonal Trading,* Wiley, New York, 1980.

Hadady, R. Earl. *Contrary Opinion,* Hadaday, Pasadena, CA, 1983.

Hadady, R. E., I. L. Finberg, and D. Rahfeldt. *Winning with the Insiders,* Weiss Research, West Palm Beach, FL, 1987.

Halberg, M. C., and V. I. West. *Patterns of Seasonal Price Variations for Illinois Farm Products,* Circular 861, University of Illinois College of Agriculture, Urbana, 1967.

Hambridge, Jay. *Dynamic Symmetry: The Greek Vase,* Yale University Press, New Haven, 1931.

Hambridge, Jay. *Practical Applications of Dynamic Symmetry,* Yale University Press, New Haven, 1938.

Hammerstrom, Dan. "Working with Neural Networks," *IEEE Spectrum,* pp. 43–45, July 1993.

Handmaker, David. "Picking Software to Trade Technically," *Commodities,* August 1982.

Harahus, David. ". . . on Market Speculation . . . ," *Harahus Analysis,* Ferndale, MI, 1977.

Harper, Henry Howard. *The Psychology of Speculation: The Human Element in Stock Market Transactions,* Fraser, Burlington, VT, 1984 (3rd printing).

Haugen, Robert A., and Josef Lakonishok. *The Incredible January Effect,* Dow Jones-Irwin, Homewood, IL, 1989.

Havens, Leston. *Making Contact,* Harvard University Press, Cambridge, MA, 1986.

Haykin, S. *Adaptive Filter Theory,* 2nd ed., Prentice Hall, Englewood Cliffs, NJ, 1991.

Haze, Van Court, Jr. *Systems Analysis: A Diagnostic Approach,* Harcourt, Brace & World, New York, 1967.

Hebb, D. O. *The Organization of Behavior,* Wiley, New York, 1949.

Hieronymus, Thomas A. *When to Sell Corn-Soybeans-Oats-Wheat,* University of Illinois College of Agriculture, Urbana, 1967.

Hieronymus, Thomas A. *Economics of Futures Trading,* Commodity Research Bureau, New York, 1971.

Higgens, James E., and Allan M. Loosigian. "Foreign Exchange Futures," in Perry J. Kaufman, ed., *Handbook of Futures Markets,* Wiley, New York, 1984.

Hildebrand, F. B. *Introduction to Numerical Analysis,* McGraw-Hill, New York, 1956.

Hill, Holliston. "Using Congestion Area Analysis to Set Up for Big Moves," *Futures,* April 1985.

Hirsch, Yale. *Don't Sell Stocks on Mondays.* Facts on File Publications, New York, 1986.

Hlawatsch, Franz, and G. Faye Bordreaux-Bartels. "Linear and Quadratic Time-Frequency Signal Representations," *IEEE Signal Processing Magazine,* vol. 9, no. 2, pp. 21–67, April 1992.

Hochheimer, Frank L., and Richard J. Vaughn. *Computerized Trading Techniques 1982,* Merrill Lynch Commodities, New York, 1982.

Howrey, E. Philip. "A Spectrum Analysis of the Long-Swing Hypothesis," *International Economic Review,* vol. 9, pp. 228–252, 1968.

Hoyne, Thomas Temple. *Speculation: Its Sound Principles and Rules for Its Practice,* Fraser, Burlington, VT, 1988.

Hsieh, David A. "Testing for Nonlinear Dependence in Daily Foreign Exchange Rates," *Journal of Business,* vol. 62, pp. 339–369, 1989.

Hull, John. *Options, Futures, and Other Derivative Securities,* 2nd ed., Prentice Hall, Englewood Cliffs, NJ, 1993.

Hurst, J. M. *The Profit Magic of Stock Transaction Timing,* Prentice Hall, Englewood-Cliffs, NJ, 1970.

Hutson, Jack K. "Good TRIX," *Technical Analysis of Stocks and Commodities,* July 1983.

Hutson, Jack K. "Using Fourier," *Technical Analysis of Stocks and Commodities,* January 1983.

Hutson, Jack K. "Filter Price Data: Moving Averages Versus Exponential Moving Averages," *Technical Analysis of Stocks and Commodities,* May/June 1984.

Hutson, Jack K. "Elements of Charting," *Technical Analysis of Stocks and Commodities,* March 1986.

Jiler, William L. *Forecasting Commodity Prices With Vertical Line Charts,* Commodity Research Bureau, New York, 1966.

Jiler, William L. *Volume and Open Interest: A Key to Commodity Price Forecasting,* Commodity Research Bureau, New York, 1967.

Johnson, Charles F. "Stochastic Oscillator Program for the HP-41C(V)," *Technical Analysis of Stocks and Commodities,* September/October 1984.

Johnson, M. *The Random Walk and Beyond,* Wiley, New York, 1988.

Jolliffe, I. T. *Principal Component Analysis,* Springer-Verlag, Berlin, 1986.

Kannerman, Daniel, and Amos Tversky. "Choices, Values, and Frames," *American Psychologist,* vol. 39, no. 4, pp. 341–350, April 1984.

Karlin, S., and H. M. Taylor. *A First Course in Stochastic Processes,* 2nd ed., Academic Press, New York, 1975.

Kaufman, Perry J. "Market Momentum Re-examined," unpublished article, November 1975.

Kaufman, Perry J. *Technical Analysis in Commodities,* Wiley, New York, 1980.

Kaufman, Perry J. "Safety-Adjusted Performance Evaluation," *Journal of Futures Markets,* vol. 1, 1981.

Kaufman, Perry J. *Handbook of Futures Markets,* Wiley, New York, 1984.

Kaufman, Perry J. "Technical Analysis," in Nancy H. Rothstein, ed., *The Handbook of Financial Futures,* McGraw-Hill, New York, 1984.

Kaufman, Perry J. "High-Tech Trading," *Futures and Options World,* London, September 1985.

Kaufman, Perry J. "Moving Averages and Trends," in Todd Lofton, ed., *Trading Tactics: A Livestock Futures Anthology,* Chicago Mercantile Exchange, 1986.

Kaufman, Perry J. *The New Commodity Trading Systems and Methods,* Wiley, New York, 1987.

Kaufman Perry J., and Kermit C. Zieg, Jr. "Measuring Market Movement," *Commodities Magazine,* May 1974.

Kelly, J. L. "A New Interpretation of Information Rate," *Bell System Technical Journal,* vol. 35, pp. 917–926, 1956.

Keltner, Chester W. *How to Make Money in Commodities,* The Keltner Statistical Service, Kansas City, MO, 1960.

Kemeny, John G., and Laurie Snell. *Finite Markov Chains,* Springer-Verlag, New York, 1976.

Kemeny John G., and Thomas E. Kurtz. *Basic Programming,* 2nd ed., Wiley, New York, 1971.

Kendall, Maurice, and J. Keith Ord. *Time Series,* 3rd ed., Edward Arnold, Sevenoaks, Kent, England, 1993.

Kepka, John F. "Trading with ARIMA Forecasts," *Technical Analysis of Stocks and Commodities,* May 1983.

Kindleberger, Charles P. *Manias, Panics, and Crashes,* Wiley, New York, 1996.

Klein, Frederick C., and John A. Prestbo. *News and the Market,* Henry Regnery, Chicago, 1974.

Kleinfield, Sonny. *The Traders,* Holt, Reinhart & Winston, New York, 1983.

Knight, Sheldon. "Tips, Tricks and Tactics for Developing Trading Systems," *Futures,* vol. XXII, no. 1, pp. 38–40, January 1993.

Knuth, Donald E. *The Art of Computer Programming,* vol. 2, *Seminumeric Algorithms,* Addison-Wesley, Reading, MA, 1971.

Koeckelenberger, Andre. Sunspot Index Data Center, 3 Avenue Circulaire, 1180, Bruxelles, Belgium.

Kolb, Robert W. *Options: The Investor's Complete Toolkit,* New York Institute of Finance, New York, 1991.

Kolmogorov, A. *Foundations of the Theory of Probability* (transl. N. Morrison), Chelsea, New York, 1956.

Korenberg, Michael J., and Larry D. Paarmann. "Orthogonal Approaches to Time Series Analysis and System Identification," *IEEE Signal Processing Magazine,* vol. 8, no. 3, pp. 29–43, July 1991.

Kroll, Stanley. *The Professional Commodity Trader,* Harper & Row, New York, 1974.

Kroll, Stanley, and Irwin Shishko. *The Commodity Futures Guide,* Harper & Row, New York, 1973.

Krutsinger, Joe. *Trading Systems Toolkit,* Probus Publishing Co., Chicago, 1994.

Kunz, Kaiser S. *Numerical Analysis,* McGraw-Hill, New York, 1957.

Labys, Walter C. *Dynamic Commodity Models: Specification, Estimation, and Simulation,* Lexington Books, Lexington, MA, 1973.

Lambert, Donald R. "Commodity Channel Index: Tool for Trading Cyclic Trends," *Commodities*, 1980 (reprinted in *Technical Analysis of Stocks and Commodities,* July 1983).

Lambert, Donald R. "The Market Directional Indicator," *Technical Analysis of Stocks and Commodities,* November/December 1983.

Lambert, Donald R. "Exponentially Smoothed Moving Averages," *Technical Analysis of Stocks and Commodities,* September/October 1984.

Lane, George C. "Lane's Stochastics," *Technical Analysis of Stocks and Commodities,* May/June 1984.

Larrain, Maurice. "Testing Chaos and Nonlinearities in T-Bill Rates," *Financial Analysts Journal,* vol. 47, no. 5, pp. 51–62, September/October 1991.

Lashonishok, Josef, and Edwin Maberly. "The Weekend Effect: Trading Patterns of Individual and Institutional Investors," *Journal of Finance,* vol. XLV, no. 1, pp. 231–243, March 1990.

Le Beau and Lucas, *Computer Analysis of the Futures Market,* Business One Irwin, Homewood, IL, 1992.

Le Bon, Gustave. *The Crowd: A Study of the Popular Mind.* Cherokee, Atlanta, GA, 1982.

Lefèvre, Edwin. *Reminiscences of a Stock Operator,* Wiley, New York, 1994 (originally published in 1923 by George H. Doran Co., New York).

Livermore, Jesse L. *How to Trade in Stocks,* Duell, Sloan & Pearce, New York, 1940.

Loeb, Gerald M. *The Battle for Investment Survival,* Wiley, New York, 1996 (originally published by Simon & Schuster).

Lofton, Todd. "Chartists Corner," *Commodities Magazine,* December 1974 (two series of articles).

Lofton, Todd. "Moonlight Sonata," *Commodities Magazine,* July 1974.

Lofton, Todd. "Trading Tactics: A Livestock Futures Anthology," *Chicago Mercantile Exchange,* 1986.

Lorenz, H. W. *Nonlinear Dynamical Economics and Chaotic Motiom,* Lecture Notes in Economics and Mathematical Systems No. 334, Springer-Verlag, Berlin, 1989.

Luce, R. Duncan, and Howard Raiffa. *Games and Decisions,* Wiley, New York, 1957.

Luenberger, D. G. *Introduction to Linear & Nonlinear Programming,* Addison-Wesley, Reading, MA, 1973.

Lukac, Louis P., G. Wade Brorsen, and Scott H. Irwin. *Similarity of Computer Guided Technical Trading Systems, CSFM-124,* Working Paper Series, Columbia Futures Center, Columbia University Business School, New York, March 1986.

Mackay, C. *Extraordinary Popular Delusions and Madness of Crowds,* Noonday Press, New York, 1974 (reprint of 19th century ed.); Barnes & Noble, New York, 1993.

Macon, Nathaniel. *Numerical Analysis,* Wiley, New York, 1963.

Marowitz, Harry. *Portfolio Selection: Efficient Diversification of Investments,* Wiley, New York, 1964.

Marple, S. Lawrence, Jr. *Digital Spectral Analysis,* Prentice Hall, Englewood Cliffs, NJ, 1987.

Mart, Donald S. *The Master Trading Formula,* Winsor Books, Brightwaters, NY, 1981.

Martin, Francis F. *Computer Modeling and Simulation,* Wiley, New York, 1968.

Mathews, V. John. "Adaptive Polynomial Filters," *IEEE Signal Processing Magazine,* vol. 8, no. 3, pp. 10–26, July 1991.

Maxwell, Joseph R., Sr. *Commodity Futures Trading with Moving Averages,* Speer, Santa Clara, CA, 1974.

McClelland, James L., and David E. Rumelhart. *Explorations in Parallel Distributed Processing,* MIT Press, Cambridge, MA, 1988.

McClish, D. K. "Comparing the Areas Under More than Two Independent ROC Curves," *Medical Decision Making,* vol. 7, pp. 149–155, 1987.

McCulloch, W. S., and W. H. Pitts. "A Logical Calculus of Ideas Immanent in Nervous Activity," *Bulletin of Mathematical Biophysics,* vol. 5, pp. 115–133, 1943.

McKinsey, J. C. C. *Introduction to the Theory of Games,* McGraw-Hill, New York, 1952.

McQueen, G., and S. Thorley. "Are Stock Returns Predictable? A Test Using Markov Chains," *Journal of Finance,* vol. XLVI, no. 1, p. 239, March 1990.

Mendenhall, William, and James E. Reinmuth. *Statistics for Management and Economics,* 2nd ed., Duxbury Press, North Scituate, MA, 1974.

Merrill, Arthur A. *Behavior of Prices on Wall Street,* The Analysis Press, Chappaqua, NY, 1966.

Miller, R. M. *Computer-aided Financial Analysis.* Addison-Wesley, Reading, MA, 1990.

Mills, Frederick Cecil. *Statistical Methods,* Henry Holt, New York, 1924.

Montgomery, Douglas C., and Lynwood A. Johnson. *Forecasting and Time Series,* McGraw-Hill, New York, 1976.

Morney, M. J. "On the Average and Scatter," in James R. Newman, ed., *The World of Mathematics,* vol. 3, Simon & Schuster, New York, 1956.

Murphy, John J. *Technical Analysis of Futures Markets,* New York Institute of Finance, New York, 1986.

Neil, Humphrey. *Tape Reading and Market Tactics,* Neil Letters of Contrary Opinion, Saxtons River, 1959 (reprint edition).

Neil, Humphrey. *The Art of Contrary Thinking,* The Caxton Printers, Caldwell, OH, 1960.

Neil, Humphrey. *The Ruminator,* Caxton Printers, Caldwell, OH, 1975.

Nelson, S. A. *The ABC of Stock Speculation,* Fraser, Burlington, VT, 1964.

Newbold, Paul. *Statistics for Business and Economics,* 2nd ed., Prentice Hall, Englewood Cliffs, NJ, 1988.

Nison, Steve. *Japanese Candlestick Charting Techniques,* New York Institute of Finance, New York, 1991.

Notis, Steve. "How to Gain an Edge with a Filtered Approach," *Futures Magazine,* September 1989.

NYIF. *Futures: A Personal Seminar,* New York Institute of Finance, New York, 1989.

Oster, Merrill J. "How Millionaires Trade Commodities," *Commodities Magazine,* March/April 1976.

Oster, Merrill J., et al. *How to Multiply Your Money,* Investors Publications, Cedar Falls, IA, 1979.

Pacelli, Albert Peter. *The Speculators Edge,* Wiley, New York, 1989.

Pardo, Robert. *Design, Testing, and Optimization of Trading Systems,* Wiley, New York, 1992.

Parker, D. B. "LE: Learning Logic," *Technical Report TR-47,* Center for Computational Research in Economics and Management Science, MIT, Cambridge, MA, 1985.

Parker, Derek, and Julia Paricora. *The Complete Astrologer,* McGraw-Hill, New York, 1971.

Paulos, John Allen. *Innumeracy: Mathematical Illiteracy and Its Consequences,* Vintage Press, New York, 1988.

Perrine, Jack. "Tarus the Bullish," *Commodities Magazine,* September 1974.

Peters, Edgar E. *Chaos and Order in the Capital Markets,* 2nd ed., Wiley, New York, 1996.

Plummer, Tony. *Forecasting Financial Markets,* Kegan Paul, London, 1989.

Poulos, E. Michael. "The Moving Average as a Trading Tool," *Commodities Magazine,* September 1973.

Poulos, E. Michael. "Futures According to Trend Tendency," *Technical Analysis of Stocks and Commodities,* vol. 10, no. 1, p. 61, January 1992.

Powers, Mark J. *Getting Started in Commodity Futures Trading,* Investors Publications, Waterloo, IA, 1975.

Prechter, Robert R., Jr. *The Major Works of R. N. Elliott,* New Classics Library, Chappaqua, NY, ca. 1980.

Prechter, Robert R., Jr. "Computerizing Elliott," *Technical Analysis of Stocks and Commodities,* July 1983.

Prechter, Robert R., Jr., David Weiss, and David Allman. "Forecasting with the Elliott Wave Principle," in Todd Lofton, ed., *Trading Tactics: A Livestock Futures Anthology,* Chicago Mercantile Exchange, Chicago, 1986.

Press, William H., Saul A. Teukolsky, William T. Vetterling, and Brian P. Flannery. *Numerical Recipes,* 2nd ed., Cambridge University Press, Cambridge, England, 1992.

Priestley, Maurice B. *Spectral Analysis and Time Series,* Academic Press, London, 1981.

Priestley, Maurice B. *Nonlinear and Nonstationary Time Series Analysis,* Academic Press, London, 1988.

Pring, Martin J. *Technical Analysis Explained,* 3rd ed., McGraw-Hill, New York, 1991.

Reiman, Ray. "Handicapping the Grains," *Commodities Magazine,* April 1975.

Resinkoff, H. L. "Foundations of Arithmeticum Analysis: Compactly Supported Wavelets and the Wavelet Group," Aware Report AD890507.1, Aware, Inc., One Memorial Drive, Cambridge, MA, 1989.

Rhea, Robert. *The Dow Theory,* Barron's, New York, 1932.

Rioul, Oliver, and Martin Vetterli. "Wavelets and Signal Processing," *IEEE Signal Processing Magazine,* vol. 8, no. 4, pp. 14–38, October 1991.

Rissanen, J. *Stochastic Complexity in Statistical Inquiry,* World Scientific, Singapore, 1989.

Rockwell, Charles S. "Normal Backwardation, Forecasting, and the Returns to Commodity Futures Traders," *Food Research Institute Studies,* vol. VII, 1967 Supplement, Stanford University Press, Stanford, CA, 1967.

Rorschach, Herman. *Psychodiagnostics,* Grune & Stratton, New York, 1942.

Rosenblatt, F. *Principles of Neurodynamics,* Sparten Press, Washington DC, 1961.

Rothstein, Nancy H. *The Handbook of Financial Futures,* McGraw-Hill, New York, 1984.

Ruckdeschel, F. R. *BASIC Scientific Subroutines,* vol. 1, Byte/McGraw-Hill, Petersborough, NH, 1981.

Ruckdeschel, F. R. *BASIC Scientific Subroutines,* vol. 2, Byte/McGraw-Hill, Peterborough, NH, 1983.

Ruelle, David. "Deterministic Chaos, the Science and the Fiction," *Proceedings of the Royal Society of London A,* vol. 427, pp. 241–248, 1990.

Rutterford, Janette. *Introduction to Stock Exchange Investment,* Macmillan, London, 1985.

Savit, Robert. "Nonlinearities and Chaotic Effects in Options Prices," *Journal of Futures Markets,* vol. 9, pp. 507–518, 1989.

Savit, Robert. "Chaos on the Trading Floor," *New Scientist,* p. 48, 11 August 1990.

Schabacker, R. W. *Stock Market Theory and Practice,* B. C. Forbes, New York, 1930.

Schabacker, R. W. *Stock Market Profits,* B.C. Forbes, New York, 1934.

Schetzen, M. *The Voltera and Weiner Theory of Nonlinear Systems,* Wiley, New York, 1980.

Schiller, Robert J. *Market Volatility,* MIT Press, Cambridge, MA, 1989.

Schirding, Harry. "Stochastic Oscillator," *Technical Analysis of Stocks and Commodities,* May/June 1984.

Schmerken, I. "Wall Street's Elusive Goal, Computers That Think Like Pros," *Wall Street Computer Review,* vol. 7, pp. 61–69, June 1990.

Schutzman, Fred G. "Smoothing over Rate of Change: New Twist to Old Study," *Futures Magazine,* April 1991.

Schwager, Jack D. *A Complete Guide to the Futures Markets,* Wiley, New York, 1984.

Schwager, Jack D. "Risk and Money Management," in Perry J. Kaufman, ed., *Handbook of Futures Markets,* Wiley, New York, 1984.

Schwager, Jack D. *Market Wizards: Interviews with Top Traders,* New York Institute of Finance, Simon & Schuster, New York, 1989.

Schwager, Jack D. "Selecting the Best Futures Price Series for Computer Testing," *Technical Analysis of Stocks and Commodities,* vol. 10, no. 10, pp. 65–71, October 1992.

Seidel, Andrew D., and Phillip M. Ginsberg. *Commodities Trading,* Prentice Hall, Englewood Cliffs, NJ, 1983.

Selden, G. C. *Psychology of the Stock Market,* Fraser, Burlington, VT, 1986.

Shanno, D. F., and Kang-Hoh Phua. "Matrix Conditioning and Nonlinear Optimization," *Mathematical Programming,* vol. 14, pp. 149–160, 1978.

Shapiro, Roy. "Why Johnny Can't Sell Losers: Psychological Roots," unpublished article, 1991.

Shaw, John E. B. *A Professional Guide to Commodity Speculation,* Parker, West Nyack, NY, 1972.

Sklarew, Arther. *Techniques of a Professional Commodity Chart Analyst,* Commodity Research Bureau, New York, 1980.

Smith, Adam. *The Money Game,* Random House, New York, 1967.

Sokoloff, Kiril. *The Thinking Investor's Guide to The Stock Market,* McGraw-Hill, New York, 1978.

Sperandeo, Victor, with Sullivan T. Brown. *Trader Vic—Methods of a Wall Street Master,* Wiley, New York, 1991.

Springer, Clifford H., Robert E. Herlihy, and Robert I. Beggs. *Advanced Methods and Models,* Irwin, Homewood, IL, 1965.

Springer, Clifford H., Robert E. Herlihy, and Robert I. Beggs. *Probalistic Models,* Irwin, Homewood IL, 1968.

Springer, Clifford H., Robert E. Herlihy, and Robert I. Beggs. *Statistical Annual,* Chicago Board of Trade, Chicago, 1969–1975 editions.

Steidlmayer, J. Peter, and Kevin Koy. *Markets & Market Logic,* Porcupine Press, Chicago, 1986.

Steinberg, Jeanette Nofri. "Timing Market Entry and Exit," *Commodities Magazine,* September 1975.

Strahm, Norman D. "Preference Space Evaluation of Trading System Performance," in Perry J. Kaufman, ed., *Handbook of Futures Markets,* Wiley, New York, 1984.

Taylor, George Douglass. *The Taylor Trading Technique,* Lilly, Los Angeles, 1950.

Taylor, Robert Joel. "The Major Price Trend Directional Indicator," *Commodities Magazine,* April 1972.

Taylor, S. J. *Modeling Financial Time Series,* Wiley, Chichester, England, 1986 (reprinted 1994).

Taylor, William T. "Fourier Spectral Analysis," *Technical Analysis of Stocks and Commodities,* July/August 1984.

Teweles, R. J., and F. J. Jones. *The Futures Game,* 2nd ed., McGraw-Hill, New York, 1987.

Teweles, Richard J., Charles V. Harlow, and Herbert L. Stone. *The Commodity Futures Game, Who Wins? Who Uses? Why?* McGraw-Hill, New York, 1974.

Tharp, Van. *Investment Psychology Guides,* Investment Psychology Consulting, Cary, NC, 1990.

Theil, Charles, and R. E. Davis. *Point and Figure Commodity Trading: A Computer Evaluation,* Dunn & Hargitt, West Lafayette, IN, 1970.

Thiriea, H., and S. Zionts, eds. *Multiple Criteria Decision Making,* Springer-Verlag, Berlin, 1976.

Thompson, J. M. T., and H. B. Stewart. *Nonlinear Dynamics and Chaos,* Wiley, Chichester, England, 1986.

Thompson, Jesse H. "The Livermore System," *Technical Analysis of Stocks and Commodities,* May 1983.

Thompson, Jesse H. "What Textbooks Never Tell You," *Technical Analysis of Stocks and Commodities,* November/December 1983.

Thorp, Edward O., *Beat the Dealer,* Vintage, New York, 1966.

Thorp, Edward O., *The Mathematics of Gambling.* Gambling Times Press, Van Nuys, CA, 1984.

Thorp, Edward O., and Sheen T. Kassouf. *Beat the Market: A Scientific Stock Market System,* Random House, New York, 1967.

Thurlow, Bradbury K. *Rediscovering the Wheel: Contrary Thinking and Investment Strategy,* Fraser, Burlington, VT, 1981.

Tippett, L. C. "Sampling and Standard Error," *The World of Mathematics,* vol. 3, James R. Newman, ed., Simon & Schuster, New York, 1956.

Tong, Howell. *Nonlinear Time Series: A Dynamical System Approach,* Oxford University Press, Oxford, 1990.

Tong, Howell, and K. S. Lim. "Threshold Autoregression, Limit Cycles and Cyclical Data," *Journal of the Royal Statistical Society,* vol. B42, pp. 245–292, 1980.

Townsend, Robert. *Up the Organization,* Knopf, New York, 1970.

Trading Strategies, Futures Systems International, Tucson, AZ, 1984.

Train, John. *The Money Masters,* Harper & Row, New York, 1980.

Turner, Dennis, and Stephen H. Blinn. *Trading Silver—Profitability,* Arlington House, New Rochelle, NY, 1975.

Twelve Steps and Twelve Traditions, Alcoholics Anonymous World Services, New York, 1952.

Vaga, Tonis. "The Coherent Market Hypothesis," *Financial Analysts Journal,* vol. 46, no. 6, pp. 36–49, November/December 1990.

Vince, Ralph. *Portfolio Management Formulas,* Wiley, New York, 1990.

Vince, Ralph. *The Mathematics of Money Management,* Wiley, New York, 1992.

Von Neumann, John, and Oskar Morgenstern. *Theory of Games and Economic Behavior,* Princeton University Press, Princeton, NJ, 1953 (first published 1943).

Wallich, Paul. "Wavelet Theory: An Analysis Technique That's Creating Ripples," *Scientific American,* pp. 34–35, January 1991.

Warren, Anthony. "A Mini Guide to Fourier Spectrum Analysis," *Technical Analysis of Stocks and Commodities,* January 1983.

Warren, Anthony. "Fourier Analysis! In a Nutshell; Faster and Better," *Technical Analysis of Stocks and Commodities,* December 1983.

Warren, Anthony. "An Introduction to Maximum Entropy Method (MEM) Technical Analysis," *Technical Analysis of Stocks and Commodities,* February 1984.

Warren, Anthony. "Optimizing the Maximum Entropy Method," *Technical Analysis of Stocks and Commodities,* March/April 1984.

Warren, Anthony, and Jack K. Hutson. "Finite Impulse Response Filter," *Technical Analysis of Stocks and Commodities,* May 1983.

Waters, James J., and Larry Williams. "Measuring Market Momentum," *Commodities Magazine,* October 1972.

Watling, T. F., and J. Morley. *Successful Commodity Futures Trading,* Business Books, London, 1974.

Watson, Donald S., and Mary A. Holman. *Price Theory and Its Uses,* 4th ed., Houghton Mifflin, Boston, 1977.

Waxenberg, Howard K. "Technical Analysis of Volume," *Technical Analysis of Stocks and Commodities,* March 1986.

Weigand, Andreas S., Bernardo A. Huberman, and David E. Rumelhart. "Back-propagation, 'Weight-Elimination and Time Series Prediction.' Connfectionist Models," in D. S. Touretzky et al., eds., *Proceedings of the 1990 Summer School,* Kaufmann, San Mateo, CA, 1991.

Weiss, Eric. "Applying ARIMA Forecasts," *Technical Analysis of Stocks and Commodities,* May 1983.

Weiss, Eric. "ARIMA Forecasting," *Technical Analysis of Stocks and Commodities,"* January 1983.

Weiss, Sholom M., and Casimer A. Kulikowski. *Computer Systems That Learn,* Kaufmann, San Mateo, CA, 1991.

Widrow, B., and S. D. Sterns. *Adaptive Signal Processing,* Prentice Hall, Englewood Cliffs, NJ, 1985.

Wilder, J. Welles, Jr. *New Concepts in Technical Trading,* Trend Research, Greensboro, NC, 1978.

Wilder, J. Welles, Jr. *Chart Trading Workshop 1980.* Trend Research, Greensboro, NC, 1980.

Williams, Edward E., and M. Chapman Findlay III. *Investment Analysis,* Prentice Hall, Englewood Cliffs, NJ, 1974.

Williams, Frank J. *If You Must Speculate, Learn the Rules,* Fraser, Burlington, VT, 1981 (2nd printing).

Williams, J. D. *The Complete Strategyst,* McGraw-Hill, New York, 1966.

Williams, Larry R. *The Secret of Selecting Stocks,* Conceptual Management, Carmel Valley, CA, 1972.

Williams, Larry R. *How I Made One Million Dollars . . . Last Year . . . Trading Commodities,* Conceptual Management, Carmel Valley, CA, 1973.

Williams, Larry. "The Ultimate Oscillator," *Technical Analysis of Stocks and Commodities,* August 1985.

Williams, Larry, and Charles Lindsey. *The Trident System,* Lindsey, O' Brien, Thousand Oaks, CA, 1975 (a report).

Williams, Larry, and Michelle Noseworthy. "How Seasonal Influences Can Help You Trade Commodities," *Commodities Magazine,* October 1976.

Winski, Joseph N. "A Sure Thing?" in *The Dow Jones Commodities Handbook 1977,* Dow-Jones Books, Princeton, NJ, 1977.

Wolf, H. J. *Studies in Stock Speculation,* Fraser, Burlington, VT, 1984 (3rd printing).

Wolf, H. J. *Studies in Stock Speculation,* vol. II, Fraser, Burlington, VT, 1985 (3rd printing).

Working, Holbrook. "Test of a Theory Concerning Floor Trading on Commodity Exchanges," *Food Research Institute Studies,* vol. VIII, *1967 Supplement,* Stanford University Press, Stanford, CA, 1967.

Wyckoff, Richard D. "How I Trade and Invest in Stocks & Bonds," *The Magazine of Wall Street,* New York, 1924.

Wyckoff, Richard D. *Wall Street Ventures and Adventures Through Forty Years,* Harper & Brothers, New York, 1930.

Wyckoff, Richard D. *Stock Market Technique, Number One,* Wyckoff, New York, 1933.

Wyckoff, Richard D. *The Richard D. Wyckoff Method of Trading and Investing in Stocks,* Wyckoff Associates, Inc., Park Ridge, IL, 1936 (originally published 1931).

Wyckoff, Richard D. *The Psychology of Stock Market Timing,* Prentice Hall, Englewood Cliffs, NJ, 1968 (5th printing).

Wyckoff, Richard D. *Jesse Livermore's Methods of Trading in Stocks,* Windsor
  Books, Brightwaters, NY, 1984.
Zieg, Kermit C., Jr., and Kaufman, Perry J. *Point and Figure Commodity Trad-
  ing Techniques,* Investors Intelligence, Larchmont, NY, 1975.
Ziemba, William T. "A Better Simulation: The Mathematics of Gambling,"
  Gambling Times, June 1987.

INDEX

Accordion
    Fibonacci, 61, 93–96, 100, 110
    Gann's series, 103
Acquisitions, announcement of, 13
Advance–consolidation–advance pattern,
    78–79, 81
Advance/Decline Index, 130
ADX, 74–76
ADXR, 74, 76
Algorithms, genetic, 131
Announcements, price movement and,
    12–13
Artificial neural networks (ANNs),
    128–130
Astrology, Bradley model of market
    forecasting and, 119–121
Automobile industry, 8, 12

Bands, stop-loss points, 113–115
Bar charts, 48
Basing pattern, 36
Bearish trends
    candlesticks, 49–50
    moving average and, 48
Bollinger bands
    defined, 40
    stop-loss points, 113, 115, 133
Box size, point-and-figure charts, 52
Bradley model of market forecasting
    applications of, 125, 133
    defined, 119–120
    Dow Jones Industrial Average,
        relationship with, 121–124
    example of, 134–135
    1994 forecasts, 121, 124
Brain, neural networks vs., 128–130

Bullish trends
    candlesticks, 49, 51
    trend channels, 38
Buy orders, price movement and, 2, 55

Caliper
    Fibonacci, 62, 137–140
    Nature's Pulse program, 93–94
Candlesticks
    application of, 48–49, 133
    types of, illustrations, 50–51
Carolan spiral calendar, 105
Channels
    application of, 133
    moving-average, 39–40
    Raff, 40–43
    support and resistance levels, 37–38
    trend, 38–39
Chart analysis, 4
Charts/charting techniques, 48–54
Close ("tight") stop, 107
Clustering, Fibonacci numbers, 95, 115, 133
Commodities, seasonality and, 18
Computer software programs. *See also*
    Bradley model of market forecasting
    G.E.T. 5.0™, 21
    Metastock™, 18, 20, 22
    Nature's Pulse program, 93–94, 98
Consolidation pattern, 77–78
Corn futures, 8
Crowd psychology, impact of, 1–2, 55
Currencies, linkages among, 12
Cycle lines, 19, 22, 25–26
Cycles, generally
    analysis, 5, 18–19, 138–139
    conventional, 17–19, 133

Delta phenomenon, 86, 120
Deutsche mark, currency linkages, 12
−DI/+DI, 74
Directional movement, 74
Displaced moving average, 44–46
Divergences
  application of, 133
  oscillators, 65–67
Divergent analysis
  defined, 65–67
  of stochastic oscillators, 73
Dollar, currency linkages, 12
Double bottom pattern, 83–84, 133
Double top pattern, 84
Downtrends, patterns in, 80
Downward gap, 2–3
Dual moving average, 45, 47–48
Duration, 5

Earnings, impact of, 12–13
Elliott waves
  analysis, 56–62
  application of, 133
  defined, 54–55
  idealized, 55
Events, types of
  Monday phenomenon, 86
  moons, full and new, 86
  options expiration, 86

Federal Reserve, 7–8, 86–87
Feedgrain linkages, 8
Fibonacci analysis, 5
Fibonacci numbers
  applications of, generally, 134
  caliper, 137–140
  clustering, 95, 115, 133
  consolidation pattern, 80
  defined, 89
  dynamic, 98–100
  Elliott-wave analysis, 61–62
  function in technical analysis,
    generally, 92
  price level and, 98–99
  stop-loss points, 115–117
  as support and resistance, 93–96
  targeting future prices, 93
  time studies, 138–140
  timing of future changes in trend, 97
Fibonacci ratios, 90–92, 120
Fibonacci series
  defined, 90

inside, 101
outside, 101–103
Rhesus, 105–106
Fibonacci time studies, 138
Five-wave sequence, Elliott waves, 58–62
Flag pattern, 77–80, 134
Followers, 4
Fourier analysis, applications of, 19–26, 134
Franc, currency linkages, 12
Fuel oil, seasonality and, 16–17
Fundamental analysis
  application of, 7
  earnings, 12–13
  linkages, 7–12
  new products, 13

Gann analysis, 26–31, 134
Gann cyclic time analysis, 27
Gann fans, 30–31
Gann lines, 27
Gann's series, 103–105
Gaps, in price, 2–4
Genetic algorithms, 130, 132
G.E.T. 5.0™, 21
Golden section proportion series, 103
Greater Fool Theory, 1–2

Harmonics, Fourier analysis, 20, 28
Head-and-shoulders patterns, 81–84, 134
Heating oil, seasonality illustration,
  16–17
Hidden layer, in artificial neural
  networks (ANNs), 128
Hidden order in all markets, 120

Indicators
  defined, 4
  direction movement, 74–76
  moving-average, generally, 43–44
  stop-and-reversal (SAR), 111–113
Input layer, artificial neural networks
  (ANNs), 128
Inside Fibonacci series, 101–102
Interest rates, market volatility and, 7–8,
  86–87
Investor's Business Daily, 134, 136–137

Kasanjian Research, 105, 119
Kroner, currency linkages, 12

Least-squares analysis, see Regression
  analysis, 13

Line(s)
in cycle analysis, 19
Fibonacci, 95
Gann, 27, 30
regression, 13, 41–42
in resistance analysis, 36–37
supply, 36
trendlines, 36–37
trigger, 63
Linear regression analysis, 40
Linkages, 7–12
Livestock futures, 8
Loose stop, 107–108

Magnitude, of price movement, 4
Market linkages, 8, 12. *See also specific types of markets*
Market rallies, events, 87
Market timing, Fibonacci numbers and, 93
Market volatility
interest rates, 2, 86–87
prediction of, Fibonacci numbers, 97–98
Mergers, announcement of, 12–13
Metastock™, 18, 20, 22
Microsoft, 12
Momentum oscillators, 65
Monday phenomenon, 86
Moons, full and new, 86, 134
Moving-average
application of, generally, 134
channels, 39–40
convergence divergence oscillator, *see* Moving average convergence divergence oscillator (MACD)
displaced, 44–46
dual, 45, 47–48
as indicator, 43–44
illustration of, 43–45
stop-loss points, 113
Moving average convergence divergence oscillator (MACD)
application of, 63–67, 74
defined, 63
example of, 134–135
neural networks and, 130
Multiple projection, Gann analysis, 28–29

Nature's Pulse software program, 93–94, 98
Neural networks, 71, 127–130. *See also* Artificial neural networks (ANNs)

New products
announcement of, 12–13
seasonal cycles and, 18

OEX, trendlines, 41
On-balance volume (OBV), 69–71, 134
Options expiration, 86
Options trading, 5
Oscillator
directional movement, 74–76
divergences, 65–67
moving average convergence divergence (MACD), 63–67
on-balance volume (OBV), 69–71
price, 47, 64
relative strength index (RSI), 67–69
stochastic, 19, 71–73
Outside Fibonacci series, 101–103

Parabolic stops, 111–113
Patterns
double bottom, 83–84
double top, 84
flags, 77–80
head-and-shoulders, 81–84
pennant, 77–78
rectangles, 77
triangles, 77–80
triple bottoms, 84–85
triple tops, 84–85
Pennant pattern, 77–78
Point-and-figure charts, 52–54
Precious metals linkages, 8
Price gaps, *see* Gaps, in price
Price movement
earnings and, 12
gaps in, 2–3
interest rates and, 7–8
linkages, 8–12
Price oscillator, *see* Oscillator
Price targets
Fibonacci time studies, 138
importance of, 4–5
setting, technical methods
candlesticks, 48–51
channels, 37–42
Elliott waves, 54–62
Kagi, 52
moving averages, 43–48
point-and-figure charts, 52–54
Renke, 52
support and resistance, 33–36
time and, 4–5

Price-to-earnings ratios, 12
Producer Price Index, 87

Raff channels
  application of, 40–43, 134
  stop–loss points, 113
Raw %K, 71
Rectangle pattern, 77, 134
Regression analysis
  application of, 134
  illustration of, 13–15
  linear, 40
Relative strength index (RSI)
  application of, 67–69, 86, 120, 134, 137
  neural networks and, 130
  oscillators, 65
  trendlines, 70
Resistance level
  defined, 35–36
  Fibonacci numbers and, 93, 95–96
  stop-loss points, 108–109
Resistance line, 36–37
Reversal size, point-and-figure charts, 52
Rhesus, 105–106
Risk objectives, stop-loss levels, 108

Seasonality, 16–17, 27, 134
Securities analysis, selection process, 134,
  137
Selling targets, Fibonacci lines, 115–117
Sell order, Fibonacci numbers and, 115–117
Sine waves, 20
Smoothed %K, 72
Soybean futures, 8–10
Spectral analysis, 21
S&P 500, 130
Square waves, Fourier analysis, 20–21
Standard & Poor's, 13
Standard deviation, 40
Stochastic oscillator, 19, 71–73, 134
Stock market crash, of 1929, 1
Stop-and-reversal (SAR) indicator, 111–113
Stop-loss level, establishment of
  bands, 113, 115
  Fibonacci numbers and, 110–111,
    115–117
  parabolic stops, 111–113
  support levels and, 108–109
  with trendlines, 109–110
Supply line, 36

Support level
  defined, 33–35
  Fibonacci numbers and, 93, 95–96
  stop-loss level, 108
Survival of the fittest, 130, 132

Targets, see Price targets; Time targets
Technical analysis
  application of, 5, 7
  Fibonacci numbers/Fibonacci ratios in, 92
  oscillators, 67
Three-line break, 52
Time analysis, Fibonacci numbers, 99
Time targets
  importance of, 4–5
  setting, technical methods
    candlesticks, 48–51
    channels, 37–42
    Elliott waves, 54–62
    Kagi, 52
    moving averages, 43–48
    point-and-figure charts, 52–54
    Renke, 52
    support and resistance, 33–36
Trading range, 36
Trend analysis, overview of
  Fourier, 20–26
  Gann, 26–31
  regression, 13–15
  seasonality, 16–17
Trend channels, 38–39
Trendlines
  defined, 36–37
  stop-loss level, 109–110
Trends, timing of, 97
Triangle pattern, 77–80
Trigger line, 63
Triple bottom pattern, 84–85
Triple top pattern, 84–85
Triple witching, 86
Trix oscillators, 65
Tulipomania, 1–2

Uptrends, patterns in, 80
Upward breakout, 38
Upward gaps, 2–3

Yen, currency linkages, 12

Zacks, 13